On Your Bike
Somerset

Nigel Vile

COUNTRYSIDE BOOKS
NEWBURY, BERKSHIRE

COUNTRYSIDE BOOKS
3 Catherine Road
Newbury, Berkshire

To view our complete range of books,
please visit us at
www.countrysidebooks.co.uk

ISBN 1 85306 776 8

Photographs and maps by the author
Designed by Graham Whiteman
Cover photograph supplied by Cyclographic Publications

Typeset by Textype, Cambridge
Produced through MRM Associates Ltd., Reading
Printed in Italy

CONTENTS

AREA MAP SHOWING THE LOCATIONS OF THE RIDES

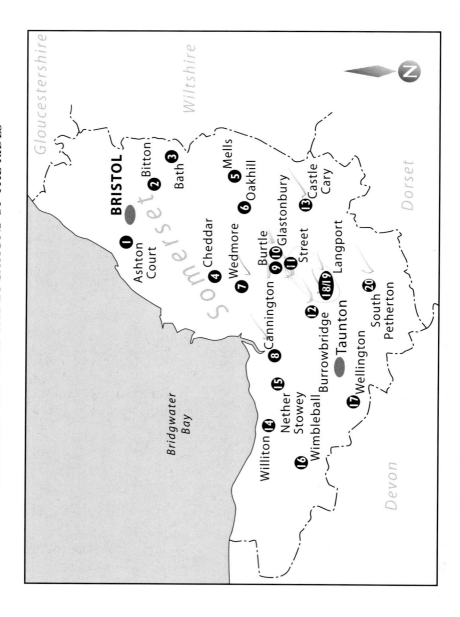

INTRODUCTION

Cycling is currently experiencing a phase of almost unrivalled popularity. Not only is this exhilarating pastime seen as being particularly healthy, it also corresponds with a time of increasing environmental awareness in society. Even city commuters are taking to the saddle in increasing numbers, a fact not unconnected with the congestion that can reduce motorised journey times to almost walking pace in Britain's major conurbations. For most of the population, however, cycling is still a leisure activity, something to be enjoyed at weekends and on holidays in the countryside.

This book of cycle rides follows quiet lanes and byways, cycle paths and tracks across Somerset, one of the most attractive counties in England. Few counties can boast such a varied array of landscape types within their boundaries, ranging from the 'excessively horizontal' peat moors around Glastonbury through to the upland heights of Exmoor, one of the country's National Parks. Add the Bristol Channel coast, the gently rolling hills of South Somerset, the limestone upland of Mendip and Wordsworth's much-loved Quantock Hills, and it is not difficult to see why Somerset is one of the country's top tourist destinations. To the north of the county – in what has been annexed to form North Somerset – lies Bristol, one of the greatest cities in the land, whilst in the adjoining authority of B&NES – that ghastly abbreviation that stands for 'Bath and North East Somerset' lies the World Heritage City of Bath, an ever-popular attraction for visitors from across the globe. All these regions feature in this collection of cycle tours, which will provide both local residents and outsiders with a fascinating insight into the heart of the West Country.

In the very north of the region, for example, a cycle path is followed through the Avon Gorge, hundreds of feet below Brunel's magnificent Clifton Suspension Bridge, whilst a few miles to the south, a spectacular downhill stretch of road is followed through the heart of Cheddar Gorge. For cyclists who prefer something just a little more leisurely, there is a gentle circuit across the Somerset Levels to the west of Glastonbury, with a similarly relaxing cycle tour following the quiet drove roads and lanes of nearby Sedgemoor in and around the historic village of Muchelney. Just in case these lowland routes are a little too easy, head west and the circuit on Exmoor in the vicinity of Wimbleball Reservoir will certainly push the body to its limits! If, on the other hand, your preference is for a gently undulating landscape with picture postcard villages and grand country houses, then head south towards Ilminster and a fine route deep in the South Somerset countryside.

This volume of cycle rides across Somerset also contains a good deal of practical information, with each cycle tour featuring:

- a brief description of the area through which the route passes
- how to get to the start of the ride
- where to park your vehicle
- which OS Landranger map to carry with you
- the nature of the terrain
- potential traffic blackspots on the route
- clear route directions integrated with a sketch map
- details on the key attractions along the way

Obviously, safety is a key factor when cycling. It is vital that your bike is roadworthy, especially if it has been in the garage throughout the winter! A general service costs just a few pounds and can save you the hours of frustration that will be suffered if something goes wrong along the way. Punctures are a fact of life for cyclists, and I would personally recommend taking a spare inner tube rather than trying to fix a flat tyre *en route*. It is also very important to wear comfortable clothing, appropriate footwear and – most importantly – a cycle helmet. Above all, however, I wish you many hours of pleasure in using this book.

Nigel Vile

GUIDE TO USING THIS BOOK

Each route is preceded by details to help you:

The **route title** tells you either the main places that you will start from or pass through, or the geographical locality in which the circuit is based. Because many cyclists will arrive at the starting point by car, each route ends where it begins. However, of course, it is possible to start and finish the route wherever you want.

The **number of miles** is the total for the ride. Most rides are along roads, which, unlike some tracks, can be ridden at any time of the year. There is also a number of routes which contain sections of off-road cycling.

The brief **introduction** to the ride gives a broad picture of where the route goes and also mentions particular features that you will see.

The **starting point** names a village or town and gives its location in the county in relation to other towns/villages and to main roads. All routes give a specific starting point within the town or village. Wherever possible, this will be a public car park.

Places for refreshments, sometimes a particular pub or tearoom is mentioned in the pre-ride information. There are also suggestions for picnic locations on some of the routes. Do not forget Paragraph 211 of the Highway Code: You MUST NOT ride under the influence of drink or drugs.

An indication is given of the **nature of the terrain** and the severity of any gradients that you will encounter, and of particularly busy main roads.

THE ROUTES

It is a good idea to read right through a route before setting out so that you note any places where you want to spend more time. The routes have been arranged according to their location in the county, rather than to their length or difficulty, so just choose ones you like the look of.

Each route is set out in numbered sections, with each number corresponding with a location on the route map. The directions have been written as clearly as possible. Instructions to turn left or right are printed in bold, like: **Turn L** at the T-junction. Instructions to continue straight over a crossroads or carry straight on are not in bold.

The directions may well include a brief comment on the route, but at the end of each circuit there is more information about **places of interest**.

The map of the county on page 4 shows where the 20 routes are situated. A simple **sketch map** accompanies each route. These maps are intended to give you a general idea of where the routes go but are not detailed enough to be route guides. The relevant OS Landranger Series map is always recommended.

SAFETY

Make sure that your bike and those of any companions – especially children – are roadworthy. This book is about routes not repairs, so seek elsewhere for do-it-yourself information or a good bike mechanic. It is unwise to set off knowing that, say, your gears are not working properly or your saddle is too low. Get things checked before you go, especially if you are riding an unfamiliar bike.

Decide in advance what you are going to do if your bike gets a puncture, and be prepared. There is no point in equipping yourself with a puncture outfit if you don't know how to use it. It might be better to take a spare inner tube – plus the tools you will need – but of course you will need to know how to deal with this, too. A mobile phone might be the best insurance policy, assuming that there is someone to phone who is prepared to come and rescue you!

Make sure you don't have things dangling off handlebars or panniers.

Locking your bike will be completely unnecessary in most of the places where these routes take you but use your common sense and lock if in doubt. This is particularly the case when stopping at a pub for lunch.

Safe cycling

Wear comfortable clothes and shoes. Wear a helmet.

Stop if you want to consult a map or this book, otherwise you may ride into a car or a ditch.

If you are with someone else or a group make sure that the pace suits everyone, and arrange that those who are ahead will stop at intervals to give the others time to catch up and get their breath back before setting off again. If you are one of the fastest, don't forget that the people behind you may not be so fit, so practised or so fond of cycling as you are. Look after them.

If you find yourself cycling in traffic you may feel safer to walk and push your bike, even if you extend your journey by half an hour.

Riding after dark is dangerous even with lights. Be very careful if you do so.

Ashton Court, Pill and the Avon Gorge

19 miles

nyone with a good knowledge of local geography would probably raise their eyebrows at the suggestion of a cycle ride from Ashton, on the fringes of Bristol, to Portbury and Pill, villages that border on Avonmouth Docks and the M5 motorway. This is admittedly a very developed and congested part of North Somerset, not the sort of area that on the surface would present ideal cycling country. The reality, however, is very surprising – and pleasantly so!

From Ashton Court, a fine estate on the south-western edge of Bristol, the route follows quiet lanes and byways through to Portbury, passing through as secluded and tranquil a landscape as might be found almost anywhere in the county. No wonder that settlements along the way – such as Abbots Leigh – have become the preserve of Bristol's wealthiest business leaders. A mile or two of potentially busy roads do have to be followed in and around Pill, before the route joins the Pill & Ashton Cyclepath. What follows, though, is a traffic-free path alongside the Avon, the highlight being the passage through the rugged cliffs of the Avon Gorge beneath Clifton Suspension Bridge.

Map: OS Landranger 172 Bristol and Bath (GR 563718).

Starting point: The parking area adjoining Ashton Court in Bristol. Follow the A369 Portishead road for 250 yards from Ashton Gate on the south-west edge of Bristol, before turning left into Kennel Lodge Road. Follow this road into the Ashton Court estate and park in the vicinity of Ashton Court itself.

Refreshments: There are a number of pubs in Pill, including the Kings Arms, which is passed at the entrance to this large suburban village, whilst at Ashton Court there is the Stables Tea Shop. If you prefer to take a packed meal, there are many fine resting spots alongside the banks of the River Avon towards journey's end.

The route: This follows, in the main, quiet lanes, cyclepaths and unmetalled tracks around the south-west fringes of Bristol. The A369 does have to be crossed east of Portway, and a short section of the same busy road does have to be negotiated at journey's end. The only other area where care does have to be exercised will be the suburban streets in Pill prior to joining the traffic-free Pill & Ashton Cyclepath. There are a few hills along the way, in the main between Ashton Court and Pill, with the final few miles between Pill and Ashton being level going alongside the River Avon.

1. Follow the estate road past Ashton Court – the Court on the left – for 150 yards to a barrier that prevents cars accessing the estate. Immediately beyond this barrier, at a junction, **fork R** towards the deer park. Follow this roadway for 250 yards to the next junction, ignore the left turn at this point and continue along the main roadway ahead as it climbs up past the deer park. Continue for ½ mile to a hilltop junction, then **turn L** to follow an unmetalled road that, beyond a barrier, crosses the hilltop. Follow this track for 1¼ miles to its junction with a lane just past Durnford Quarry, initially crossing a series of golf greens.

2. Turn R, and cycle for ¼ mile to a junction with the B3129. Cross over, and follow the lane opposite for 1 mile as it winds its way to the fringes of Abbots Leigh, then **turn L** into Manor Lane. Follow this lane for ¼ mile to a junction – opposite Staddlestone House – **turn L**, and follow a winding, hilly lane for 2 miles to St Bartholomew's church in Failand. About 150 yards past the church, **turn R** into Failand Lane – signposted to Portbury – and follow this road for 1¼ miles to the next junction. **Turn R**, and cycle into Portbury and, at the junction with the High Street, **keep R** on the main road to Portishead and the M5. In 150

Ashton Court on the edge of Bristol

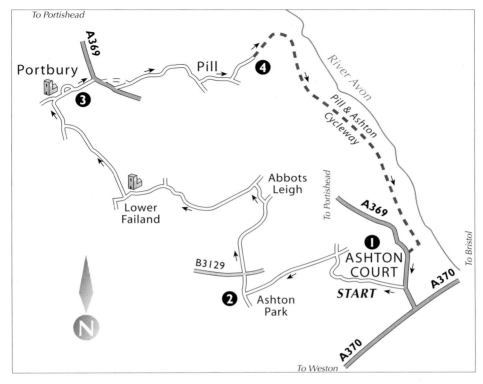

yards, **turn L** into Church Road, cycle past St Mary's church and continue along what is a 'loop' back to the main road. **Turn L**, and continue towards the A369 and Portbury.

3. Immediately before the A369, **fork R** along the path signposted 'Avon Cycleway' and continue to a crossing point across the main road. Having crossed the A369, follow the cycle path opposite to its junction with the road leading into Pill. **Turn L**, and cycle down St George's Hill into Pill. In 1¼ miles, having climbed a steep, 1-in-8 hill, **turn L** at a mini-roundabout

shortly before the Anchor Inn. Cycle down past some new housing, looking out for 'Cycle Route 41' signs. In 250 yards, **fork L** along Chapel Pill Lane; continue for ½ mile to Chapel Pill Farm and join the Pill & Ashton Cycleway beyond a kissing gate.

4. Follow this path for 3½ miles alongside the River Avon to the Clifton Suspension Bridge. In another 600 yards, at a junction at the top of a climb, **turn R** across a railway bridge and join the A369. **Turn L**, and follow this road with care, cycling down past the Avon Police Dog and Horse complex. In

350 yards, **turn R** on an awkward bend into Kennel Lodge Road – it is advisable to dismount and walk across the main road. Continue along this road for ½ mile back to the parking area by Ashton Court.

• •

ASHTON COURT

Ashton Court, with its massive 300 ft frontage, is an intriguing blend of styles ranging from Gothic and Jacobean to Tudor. There are even unsubstantiated suggestions that the south-west wing may have been the work of Inigo Jones. This was home for the Smyth family for over 400 years. Thomas Smyth, an MP in Stuart times, was one of the last landowners to employ a jester. The family fortunes diminished during the 20th century, and in 1959 the whole estate was purchased by Bristol City Council for use as a public amenity. The grounds were landscaped by Repton (1725-1818) and run to some 840 acres, included within which is a deer park.

PILL

Pill is located around a creek of the River Avon. For generations, this was home to the Pill pilots, whose job was to guide vessels from the Bristol Channel into the City Docks in Bristol. Young boys were apprenticed to relatives, the apprenticeship to become a pilot lasting for up to nine years. At high tide, the Pill – which lies just off the route – is an interesting spot, with a number of small boats bobbing up and down on the muddy water. At low tide, the expanse of grey mud is something of an acquired taste! For many years, a ferry ran across the Avon to Shirehampton, but the service was discontinued in 1970.

THE RIVER AVON

The River Avon, a mere 75 miles in length, springs to life in the Cotswold foothills above Malmesbury. From Bath to Avonmouth, the river is navigable and is extremely popular in the pleasure-boat world. West of Bristol, the Avon Gorge and Brunel's magnificent suspension bridge provide one of the region's best known landmarks. Here the river is tidal, and was the site of the last commercial traffic to work the river – sand dredgers operating out of the City Docks that would scour the Bristol Channel. Avon is in fact a common English river name, with the Bristol, Warwickshire and Hampshire versions alone being waters of national repute.

THE CLIFTON SUSPENSION BRIDGE

The bridge owes its origins to William Vick, a Bristol wine merchant who died in 1752. He left £1,000 to the city of Bristol, money which was to be invested until the magnificent sum of £10,000 resulted. Work was then to commence on a bridge that would span the Avon Gorge. Eighty years passed before any further progress was made, then a competition was held and eventually one of Brunel's designs was selected as the winning entry. Unfortunately, funds ran out by 1840 and the bridge was abandoned. Its chains were sold to the company building the Tamar Bridge, and just two lonely towers were left gazing at each other across the gorge. Following Brunel's death in 1859, a new bridge company was formed, fresh capital was raised and, on Thursday 8th December 1864, the bridge was opened. At a cost of £100,000, Bristolians were rewarded with a bridge that was 245 feet above the river and whose span was over 700 feet.

Along the Bristol and Bath Railway Path

14 miles

The Midland Railway running between Bristol and Bath was one of the unfortunate victims of the Beeching cuts of the 1960s. Freight was carried along the line for a few years following the withdrawal of passenger services, but the iron road finally closed in the early 1970s. Between 1979 and 1986 it was converted into the first purpose-built cycleway in the country, and now provides a traffic-free cycling route between the two major cities in the region.

Raised on an embankment for much of its course, the railway path brings fine views across the Avon Valley as it heads out from the former station at Bitton towards the Georgian city of Bath. To the north, the southern slopes of the Cotswolds come tumbling down towards the Avon, whilst to the south the views extend beyond Keynsham towards the distant Mendip Hills. Despite starting in South Gloucestershire, this route soon crosses the boundary into Bath and North East Somerset, and provides a perfect introduction to this corner of the county.

Map: OS Landranger 172 Bath and Bristol (GR 669703).

Starting point: The car park at Bitton station, which is now the headquarters of the Avon Valley Railway. Bitton station lies alongside the A431, midway between Bath and Bristol.

Refreshments: Available at Bitton station, whilst at Saltford the railway path passes the Bird in Hand public house. On reaching Bath, you could either chain your bicycles up at the end of the riverside path and stroll into the city for refreshments, or do battle with the city's heavy traffic! Whichever option you choose, it is literally just 200 yards into the city centre.

The route: This linear route is mainly based upon the traffic-free Bath and Bristol Railway Path. The path – a 3-metre wide tarmacked surface – follows a level course for the whole of this cycle ride. With no cars or hills to contend with, it provides a perfect family cycle excursion. On reaching the western fringes of Bath, a short section of cycling through a suburban housing area brings the route to the West Bath Riverside Path, another traffic-free section that continues into the heart of Bath.

---

1. Join the railway path at the southern end of Bitton station's car park, and follow this delightful cycle route for 5½ miles until it joins Brassmill Lane on the edge of Bath by a business park. Initially, the cycle path borders a restored section of the Midland Railway,

On the Riverside Path

before crossing the River Avon and heading out towards Saltford and the Bird in Hand public house. The cycle path then re-crosses the Avon and passes beneath the slopes of Kelston Park before reaching Brassmill Lane.

2. Head along Brassmill Lane for 600 yards until, just past the Avon Tools Hire depot, **bear R** to join the West Bath Riverside Path. Having passed the Dolphin Inn, continue alongside the river for another 1¼ miles until the path reaches the busy road network on the edge of Bath's city centre. There is a grass verge, should you wish to rest and linger awhile rather than going into the centre of Bath.

3. Retrace your steps along the riverside path and Brassmill Lane back to the Bath and Bristol Railway Path. With the hustle and bustle of the city left behind, follow the cycle route for 5½ miles, all the way back to Bitton station.

● ●

THE AVON VALLEY RAILWAY
To quote the publicity material, 'The Avon Valley Railway is more than just a train ride, offering a whole new experience for some or a nostalgic memory for others'. Known as 'The Bristol Suburban Railway Society' when it was formed in 1972, the aim of this preservation trust was to acquire and re-open the former Midland Railway line running between Bristol, Mangotsfield and Bath Green Park stations. So far, 2 miles of track have been reopened

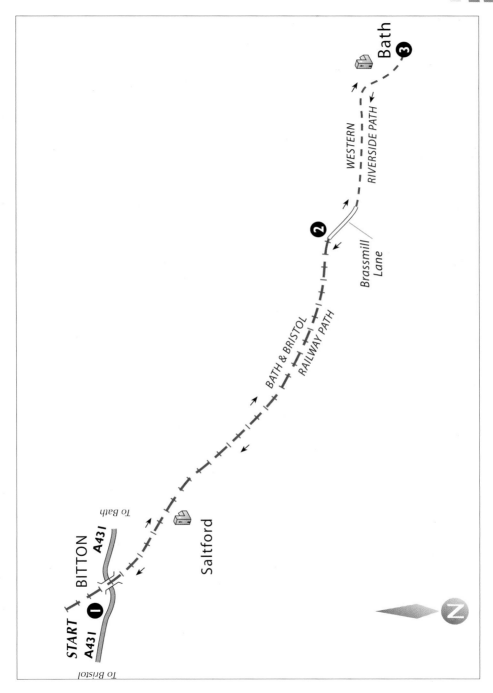

either side of the trust's headquarters at Bitton station. The line currently extends northwards to Oldland Common, where a new platform was constructed to replace the halt demolished in the 1860s, and in a southerly direction into the Avon Valley. As well as enjoying a 4-mile round trip from Bitton station, visitors can explore the former goods yard that is home to a mixture of mainline and industrial steam and diesel locomotives, as well as a number of carriages and wagons.

THE RIVER AVON

The River Avon has its beginnings deep in the southern Cotswolds, near to either Sherston or Tetbury, depending on which of two tributary streams represents the genuine source. For much of its 75-mile course, it flows through the undulating Wiltshire countryside, where its waters enhance such delightful settlements as Malmesbury, Lacock and Bradford-on-Avon. The river subsequently flows through the dramatic Limpley Stoke Valley before passing through the incomparable Georgian city of Bath and the former commercial port of Bristol. Between these two cities, the river has been navigable on a seasonal basis since time immemorial, but it was only in 1712 that an Act of Parliament was passed to create the Avon Navigation. The river was canalised between Bristol and Bath by

1727, six locks being constructed to overcome the rise of 30 feet between these two cities. Commercial traffic continued along the river until 1967, the last working barge carrying gas tar from Bath Gas Works to Crew's Hole on the outskirts of Bristol. Today, the Avon is alive with the sounds of pleasure craft, especially following the restoration of the Kennet and Avon Canal, east of Bath.

BATH

Bath has been famous as a source of healing waters since Roman times when, as Aquae Sulis, it attracted visitors from all over the empire. Following a period of decline in the Middle Ages, by the 18th century Bath was once again one of the foremost cities in the land, thanks to developer Ralph Allen, architect John Wood and society leader Richard 'Beau' Nash. It became a fashionable resort, with public buildings and residential terraces attracting such luminaries as William Pitt, Lord Clive, Thomas Gainsborough and David Livingstone. Jane Austen was but another visitor to the city; her novel Northanger Abbey painting a vivid picture of the social life of the time. The city still attracts visitors from all across the world, the Abbey church, Roman baths, Pump Room and Assembly Room being just some of the fine attractions that Bath has to offer.

Bath, Freshford and Wellow

18 miles

There is still a groundswell of opposition to the annexation of a slice of Somerset countryside into a new hybrid authority with the grandiose abbreviation of 'B&NES' – Bath and North East Somerset to you and me. This cycle tour explores a delightful corner of this recently created council area, where 'Back to Somerset' campaigns have still not disappeared from the letters columns of the local press.

Starting with a delightful stretch of towpath cycling alongside the Kennet and Avon Canal, the route's gentle nature suddenly changes into a dramatic landscape of hills and valleys that will certainly test out every sinew and muscle. Along the way are a number of quite beautiful villages and hamlets, with manor houses and churches, cottages and farmhouses all lovingly fashioned from the golden Bath stone that lends so much character to this area.

Map: OS Landranger 172 Bristol and Bath (GR 778666).

Starting point: The Kennet and Avon Canal at Bathampton. Follow the A36 Warminster road south from Bath and, one mile from the city centre, fork left along Bathampton Lane and drop down to Bathampton village. Having crossed the canal, turn immediately right into Tyning Lane and park on the roadside in the vicinity of Bathampton School.

Refreshments: There are inns at Limpley Stoke, Freshford, Hinton Charterhouse, Wellow, Midford and Monkton Combe, none of which will fail to please, whilst the George at Bathampton enjoys a quite delightful canalside location – as well as being conveniently located at journey's end. A short detour at Dundas when rejoining the canal prior to returning to Bath will bring you to the Canal Visitor Centre with its excellent café.

The route: The very busy A36 does have to be crossed on a couple of occasions along the way, whilst two short stretches of the B3110 have to be negotiated at Hinton Charterhouse and Midford. Otherwise, the route follows quiet lanes and byways, as well as a traffic-free stretch of the Kennet and Avon Canal towpath. There are a number of hills along the way, chiefly around Iford and Wellow, but do remember the old adage about what goes up having to come down again.

---

1. Cycle in a southerly direction along the Kennet and Avon Canal towpath for 3½ miles to Dundas.

On approaching Dundas, cross a bridge on the right, cycle around the wharf and over the entrance to

Iford Manor has an Italianate garden

the Somerset Coal Canal and head across Dundas aqueduct. Continue following the towpath for 1 mile to Winsley Hill overbridge.

2. Leave the towpath, **turn R** down the B3108 and pass under a railway bridge before taking the **L turn** signposted Limpley Stoke. Follow the road ahead uphill for ¾ mile to a junction at the top of Crowe Lane. **Turn L** and follow the road as it winds its way downhill for 600 yards, ignoring all side turns, to reach the inn at Freshford. Continue for 600 yards until, at the top of a climb, take the **R turn** signposted 'Unsuitable for heavy vehicles – Iford only'. Follow this lane for 1 mile into Iford, **turn R** over the Frome and follow the lane ahead for 1¼ miles up to the A36.

3. Cross the A36 with care and follow the lane opposite for ¼ mile to a junction. **Turn L** along a lane and continue for ½ mile to the B3110 in Hinton Charterhouse. **Turn R** and, in 150 yards, **turn L** just past the Stag Inn onto the road signposted to Wellow. Follow this lane for 2¼ miles to the square in Wellow by the Fox and Badger Inn. **Turn R** – signposted to Combe Hay and Bath – and follow the road to a hilltop junction in ½ mile.

4. Turn R – signposted to Twinoe –

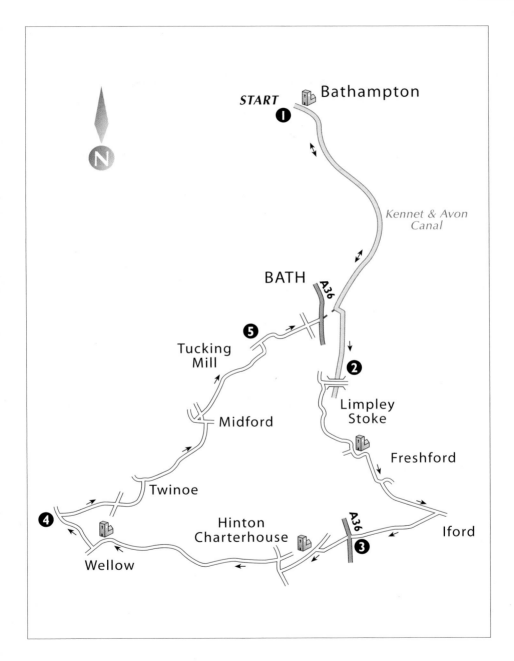

and follow the lane for 1½ miles to a junction by Middle Twinoe Farm. **Turn R**, and follow the lane for another 1½ miles across the hilltop and downhill to the B3110 in Midford. **Turn L** and, almost immediately, **turn R** up to a minor crossroads in the heart of old Midford. **Turn R**, and follow the lane for 1¼ miles to a junction on the edge of Monkton Combe, passing through Tucking Mill along the way.

5. Turn R, and cycle down through Monkton Combe and on to a crossroads in ¾ mile at the foot of Brassknocker Hill. Cross over with care and follow the lane opposite down to the A36. Cross to the drive opposite that leads down to the canal at Dundas Wharf. **Turn L**, cycle along to the bridge, cross the canal and retrace the route along the towpath back to Bathampton.

• •

THE KENNET AND AVON CANAL

Between Bathampton and Dundas, the Kennet and Avon Canal passes through arguably the finest landscape along the whole length of this fine waterway. The Avon Valley hereabouts is characterised by steep, wooded hillsides that come tumbling down to the river's edge, with the narrow valley bottom carrying not only the canal, but also the main Bristol to Southampton railway as well as the A36 trunk road to the south coast. Claverton is the site of an historic pumping station, where water is lifted from the Avon into the canal, whilst Dundas is a veritable treasure chest for industrial archaeologists. This is where the Somerset Coal Canal joined the Kennet and Avon – indeed, a short section of the coal canal has been restored for moorings and there is a consequent wharf with the inevitable warehouse and crane in situ. Dundas is also the site of the finest aqueduct in southern Britain, with a series of fine arches and Doric columns that are testimony to the skill of John Rennie, the canal's chief engineer. A short detour at Dundas will bring you to the Canal Visitor Centre, where, as well as various interpretive displays, visitors can enjoy welcome refreshment.

IFORD

Although strictly over the border in Wiltshire, Iford deserves a passing mention. This is a beautiful spot, where the Somerset Frome flows beneath an ancient bridge topped out with a fine limestone statue of Britannia. Iford Manor, whose attractive Italianate gardens complete what is a picture-perfect setting, overlooks the whole scene. Best viewed from the riverbank, the main part of the manor dates from the early 18th century; the Casita on the far right of the garden is a genuine Italian work of the 13th century, brought to Iford in 1913.

WELLOW

Wellow is best approached from Hinton Charterhouse, which is fortunately the direction from which this route enters the village. The stone cottages and houses, with their southerly aspect, can be seen in the distance clinging to the hillside, with the Wellow Brook flowing along gently in the valley below. The many attractive properties are centred upon the village square, where the excellent Fox and Badger public house – a regular entry in the *Good Pub Guide* – forms the natural focal point. At the eastern approach to the village stands St Julian's church, built in the Somerset Perpendicular style, with a majestic tower that overlooks a rolling landscape of steep hillsides and plunging valleys. A rather impressive railway

William Smith's cottage at Tucking Mill

viaduct also dominates the eastern approach to Wellow. Until the Beeching cuts of 1966, the Somerset & Dorset Railway, running from Bath Green Park to Bournemouth, ran this way. The S&D – 'swift and delightful' to its friends, 'slow and dirty' to its critics – is one of Britain's most lamented railways. It is not difficult to see why when you look at the landscape around this corner of Somerset, through which it carved a course.

TUCKING MILL

Tucking Mill may seem an inconsequential settlement – a few stone houses and little more, deep in a sylvan combe – but this is a hamlet with a deal of history. The Somerset Coal Canal, running from the Somerset Coalfield around Radstock and Paulton to Dundas, ran this way, and it was the canal's construction that brought William Smith to the area as the waterway's surveyor. 'Strata'

Smith is none other than the father of English geology, and it was whilst working on the canal in the vicinity of Tucking Mill that an exposed section of rock face planted an idea into his mind. From this flash of inspiration, Smith slowly developed the geological maps with which we are now so familiar. A rather grand property that is passed along the way bears a plaque claiming that this was the residence of William Smith when working on both the canal and his geological research. Recent research says otherwise, however. Look just beyond William Smith's alleged cottage to a rather shabby and rundown property hidden in the nearby woodland. This has been proved to be Smith's residence, but its demeanor and appearance might explain why the tourism departments – and local estate agents – prefer the plaque to be attached to the more prominent and attractive residence.

4
Cheddar and the Mendip Hills

17 miles

The Mendip Hills, an area of limestone upland, stretch across the north of the county from Weston-super-Mare to Wells and Frome. West Mendip – the focus of this cycle tour – is home to the region's best-known attractions, which include Cheddar Gorge, Wookey Hole and the rocky outcrops at Burrington Combe. Indeed, the highlight of this circuit will undoubtedly prove to be the 3-mile descent through Cheddar Gorge itself.

Along the way lie a number of towns and villages that will provide much to catch the eye. These range from Cheddar, with its plethora of tourist shops and businesses, to the remote upland hamlet of Charterhouse, with its disused lead mines that date back to Roman times and beyond. It is the natural landscape that will linger longest in the memory, however – the glorious heights of Mendip, the rock faces of Cheddar Gorge and the impressive south-facing slopes of this hill range.

Map: OS Landranger 182 Weston-super-Mare and Bridgwater (GR 461535).

Starting point: The Cliff Street car park at the southern approach to Cheddar Gorge. Leave the A371 in Cheddar village and follow the signposted road up towards Cheddar Gorge. In 300 yards, just before the Riverside Inn and Gordon's Hotel, **turn R** into the car park (fee payable).

Refreshments: Along the route, barely a couple of miles passes without a café, pub or ancient hostelry, other than the 'dry' leg of the circuit on high Mendip between Shipham and Cheddar. With this in mind, a packed lunch – to be consumed on the open ground around Charterhouse – is my personal recommendation. The added attraction is that all of the hill-work will have been completed, and it is downhill all of the way back to Cheddar.

The route: The roads and side streets in Cheddar, Axbridge, Winscombe and Shipham can be busy with local residents travelling to and from the shops and other local amenities. Short stretches of busy A and B class roads must also be used in these towns and villages, so due care should be exercised. There are also some stiff climbs along the way, including a rise of some 450 feet as the route climbs from Shipham onto the Mendip uplands. The reward is a fine downhill run through the gorge back into Cheddar.

Axbridge

1. Leave the car park, **turn R** past Gordon's Hotel, before taking a **L turn** at a mini-roundabout onto the B3135. Follow this road for 600 yards then **turn L** opposite the local Catholic church into Lower North Street. Follow this back road down to the A371. **Turn R** and, in 100 yards, by the war memorial, **turn L** along the B3151 Wedmore road. At the first turning on the right, **turn R** into the Valley Line Industrial Park and, at the end of what is a cul-de-sac, join the Valley Line Cycle Path. Follow this traffic-free route for 1¼ miles to the A371 on the edge of Axbridge. **Turn L** along this main road before taking the first **L turn** into Axbridge itself. Follow West Street out of Axbridge town centre, passing in front of the Lamb Inn, and continue for ¼ mile to a road junction. **Turn L** along what is again the A371, signposted to Taunton and Exeter, and continue to its junction with the A38.

2. Cross the A38 to follow the lane opposite, signposted to Loxton. Follow this lane for 3 miles through to Webbington, the impressive southern slopes of the Mendip Hills on the right. In Webbington, just before the road crosses the M5 motorway, **turn R** along the turning to Winscombe. Follow this road – Barton Road – for 3 miles to a junction by Brook Corner House in Winscombe. **Turn L**

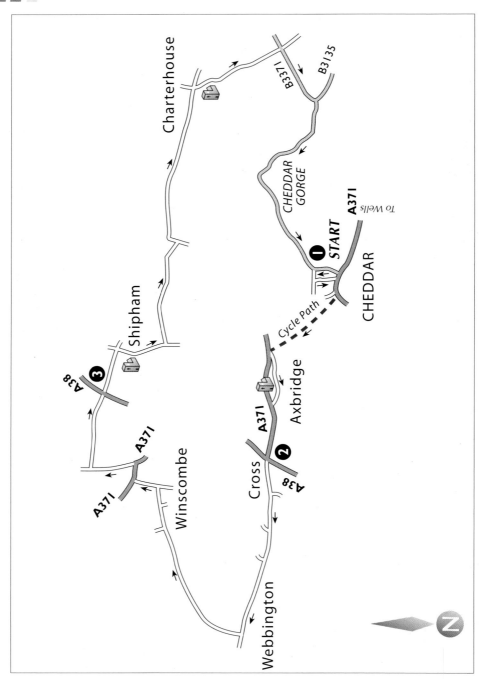

Cheddar Gorge

up to the A371, before you **turn R** to pass under a railway bridge to reach a junction in front of the Woodborough Inn. **Turn L** at this point, off the A371, and follow the road ahead for ½ mile to a right turn – Shipham Lane. **Turn R**, and follow this lane for 1¼ miles up to the A38.

3. Cross the A38 and follow the road opposite, signposted to Shipham, for ¾ mile up to a crossroads. **Turn R**, cycle through Shipham and, in ¾ mile, just before a café, take a **L turn** signposted to Charterhouse. In 2 miles, at a junction, keep on the main lane that **bears L** down to Tynings Farm, before **bearing R** and

continuing for 2½ miles to a crossroads in Charterhouse. A detour ahead will bring you to the site of the lead workings in this remote hamlet. For the main route, **turn R**, and continue for 1½ miles to a crossroads by King Down Farm. **Turn R** – the B3371 to Cheddar – and continue for 1 mile to a junction with the B3135. **Turn R**, and follow this occasionally busy road for 3 miles down through Cheddar Gorge to the Riverside Inn on the left. Immediately past this hostelry, take a **L turn** into the car park.

● ●

THE MENDIP HILLS
The Mendips, a vast limestone mass,

stretch for some 30 miles across northern Somerset from Weston-super-Mare in the west to Frome in the east. The most outstanding and most well-known features in the region are the extensive network of cliffs and underground caverns that have been carved out of the limestone over many thousands of years by the action of running water. Mendip is a bleak and lonely landscape, especially on the high ground around Charterhouse, which rises to a height of 1,067 feet above sea-level at Beacon Batch. Criss-crossed by ancient tracks and roads, the numerous tumuli and barrows testify to the historic importance of the region.

CHEDDAR GORGE

'The incline became steeper, the winding more intense. The boulders suddenly became high, vertical precipices of limestone, with tall trees growing out of them. Then it became even grander, and more awe-inspiring. In the high gale I felt certain that the rocks were going to fall on me. The cliffs assumed shapes – a lion here, a monkey there.' It is over 50 years since S P B Mais penned this vivid description of Cheddar Gorge, and the passage of time has done little to diminish what must surely rank as some of the finest inland cliff scenery in the country. The gorge was carved out by running water in centuries long past. Rainwater contains a mild solution of acid, which readily dissolves the cracks and joints found in the Mendip limestone. The cliffs rise to over 500 feet in height and are dotted with squat yew trees and whitebeam, rare alpine pennygrass and the unique Cheddar pink. The rock ledges provide nesting grounds for many jackdaws, whose squawks echo incessantly around the gorge.

CHARTERHOUSE

The OS map shows both a 'Roman Fort' and a 'Roman Settlement' at Charterhouse. What brought the Romans to this remote Mendip outpost were the local lead deposits. The lead was widely used throughout the Roman Empire, one notable function being to line the Roman baths at nearby Bath. A Roman road ran across the Mendips to Old Sarum and the south coast ports, from where the riches of Charterhouse were shipped to all points of the empire. The lead was worked as recently as the late 19th century by the Mendip Mining Company, when the chief activity was extracting lead from the plentiful Roman and medieval refuse. Today, spoil tips, horizontal flues and washing pools are quietly reverting to a more natural landscape.

AXBRIDGE

Axbridge is a town of great antiquity. In the 11th century, the settlement had its own mint and a market that brought pedlars from great distances to serve the needs of the Mendip settlers and farmers. Later in its history, the town had its own mayor and corporation, which finally disappeared in 1886. The borough records are still retained in the town, which was at one time in the hands of two lords of the manor – one was William Longsword, the other the Bishop of Bath and Wells. The town square is dominated by the imposing 15th century church of St John, in Somerset Perpendicular style. As well as a fine west porch, the nave roof holds Jacobean plasterwork constructed in an intricate series of geometric shapes. King John's Hunting Lodge will also catch the eye. This fine jettied and timber-framed merchant's house, dating from Tudor times, now houses a museum devoted to displays of local interest.

Mells, Nunney and Great Elm

13 miles

E ast of Wells, the Mendip Hills begin to lose some of their dramatic high points. There are no longer the spectacular limestone cliffs, epitomised by Cheddar Gorge, or the vast underground caverns, such as those found at Wookey. The landscape becomes rather more undulating, with gentle hills and wooded valleys and with the tourist honeypots few and far between. This is much more of a workaday countryside – with old-fashioned villages characterised by traditional farms and cottages – where quarrying is eating away at the landscape.

This cycle tour explores the countryside to the west of Frome, where, in amongst the undulations, lie a number of quite delightful settlements. In Nunney, for example, a ruinous castle overlooks the main street, whilst in Mells we find an archetypal Somerset Perpendicular church towering above the local manor house. Running through this corner of East Mendip are a number of rivers and streams whose waters have carved out a series of plunging valleys that add to the beauty along the way. There is a series of ups-and-downs to negotiate, but the effort is worth every bead of perspiration.

Map: OS Landranger 183 Yeovil & Frome (GR 728492).

Starting point: The Talbot Inn at Mells. There is ample room for roadside parking in the vicinity of this ancient hostelry. Mells lies on an unclassified road 3 miles west of Frome. Leave the A362 Frome to Radstock road 1 mile northwest of Frome, and follow the well-signposted road into Mells.

Refreshments: Along the route, there are inns and pubs in Mells, Nunney, Frome and Buckland Dinham. The Talbot Inn at Mells is a traditional coaching inn – with all the character and feel that would be expected of such an establishment – and lies most conveniently at journey's end. If you decide to carry a packed lunch with you, an excellent spot to rest and linger awhile is beside the Mells River in Great Elm, where the river's course has been utilised to create a millpond deep in Vallis Vale.

The route: Other than a brief encounter with the A362 at Buckland Dinham, this route follows generally quiet lanes and byways in the Mendip countryside east of Frome. There are a number of significant quarries in the area, however, which could mean that you might encounter the occasional lorry, particularly on sections of the ride between Mells and Nunney. There are also a number of hills along the way, especially south of Chantry and on the western approaches to Frome, as well as in Great Elm. Always remember, however, that what goes up must go down!

Mells Stream at Great Elm

1. Follow the road westwards from the Talbot Inn for ½ mile to a junction. **Turn L** – signposted to Nunney and Frome – and drop downhill into a valley bottom. Having crossed the Mells River, immediately **bear R** off the main road to follow a side lane up across Mells Green to a junction above Mells First School. **Turn R** signposted Leigh upon Mendip and Wells – and follow the road ahead for 1¼ miles to a crossroads. **Turn L** – signposted to Chantry and Frome – and, in 300 yards, at the top of a climb, **turn L** along the lane to Chantry. Follow this lane for ¾ mile to a minor crossroads just past Chantry church.

2. Turn R along a lane marked as unsuitable for heavy vehicles.

Follow this lane down into the valley bottom by Manor Farm and uphill to a junction. **Turn L**, and follow this road for 600 yards to a crossroads. Cross over and follow the road to Nunney. In 300 yards, just past Castle Hill Farm, **turn R** down into Nunney itself. Cross Nunney Brook to a junction, before taking the **L turn** to Frome. Follow this road for just over 2 miles – it eventually climbs uphill to reach the outskirts of Frome. **Turn L** at the first crossroads in the town into Oakfield Road. Head along past Oakfield School and the police station to a junction with Broadway by the Royal Oak Pub.

3. Turn R and, almost immediately, **turn L** into Egford Lane. Drop downhill for ½ mile to

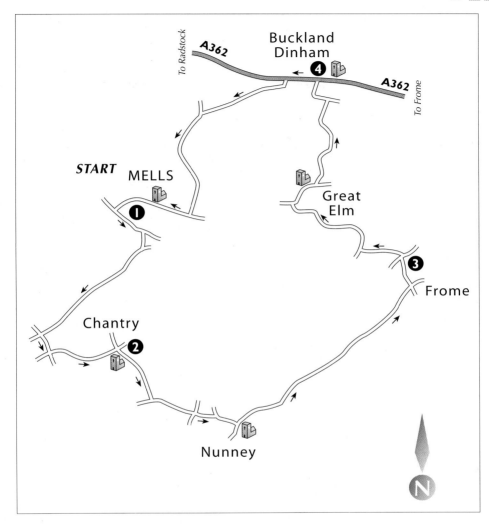

a junction, **turn R** and follow the road for
1 mile into Great Elm. Cross the Mells river and continue along the lane as it climbs steeply uphill to reach the Mells to Great Elm road. **Turn R** and follow the road for 250 yards until, just before a converted chapel, **turn L** along an unmarked lane. Follow this lane for 1 mile to

a junction just below Buckland Dinham. **Turn L**, and follow the lane uphill to the A362 and the Bell Inn in Buckland Dinham.

4. **Turn L** and, in ¼ mile, opposite a farm, **turn L** along an unmarked lane. Follow this for 1 mile across the hilltop to a junction, where you **turn L** along the road to Mells.

Follow this road for 1½ miles to a junction in Mells. **Turn R** – signposted to Coleford and Radstock – pass the village post office and follow the road back up to the Talbot Inn.

• •

MELLS

Mells is one of the prettiest villages in the whole of Somerset. The setting of the ancient manor alongside St Andrew's church is picture-postcard perfect, the whole completed by the local hostelry – the Talbot – a traditional coaching inn, and the medieval terraces of New Street. The village is forever associated with the Horner family, local legend invoking an association with the infamous nursery rhyme character. Historically, Mells formed part of the rich demesne of Glastonbury Abbey. At the time of the Dissolution, Jack Horner – a steward to the abbot – was carrying a bundle of deeds to London, when he decided to apportion certain property rights to himself. These turned out to be none other than the ownership rights to Mells Manor – and he certainly 'pulled out a plum' to quote the rhyme! St Andrew's church is a fine example of Somerset Perpendicular architecture, although visitors are drawn to the graves of the celebrities buried in the churchyard, including Siegfried Sassoon and Lady Violet Bonham-Carter.

NUNNEY

Nunney owes much of its traditional wealth to the West of England woollen industry. The Nunney Brook, which runs through the village, has been documented as a 'pavement place to wash wool' in the heyday of cloth making. Overshadowing the village are the ruinous remains of Nunney Castle, built by St John de la Mare, who crenellated this handsome fortification in 1373. It was ruined during the Civil War, when the Parliamentarians, well equipped with artillery, bombarded it to the point of surrender. The Roundheads tore out all the joists and floorboards so systematically that the place was never lived in again. Four drum towers still stand impressively inside a moat, with the sound of rooks and crows providing an evocative atmosphere to this fine ancient monument. All Saints itself was almost entirely rebuilt in the 19th century, although the 13th-century chancel still survives. Sadly, a magnificent 15th-century wagon roof disappeared in the 1950s, a victim of the deathwatch beetle.

BUCKLAND DINHAM

Set against a backdrop of low, wooded hills and fields dotted about with oak and ash, Buckland Dinham may convey the image of yet another village scattered along a main road – but there is a deal of history attached to this settlement. In the reign of Henry III, for example, a charter was granted for the village to hold a weekly market and a fair at Michaelmas, but these gatherings slowly died out, as did the local textile trade and a penchant for teasel growing. The village also stood on the fringes of the Somerset coalfield, but 19th-century attempts to find commercial deposits of 'black gold' in the area failed. A solitary chimney set in isolation in a nearby field is all that remains of this period in Buckland Dinham's history. Around the village are a number of attractive buildings, including Ebenezer Chapel, a handsome Methodist place of worship, a small lockup with a barred porthole and St Michael's church. Inside the church is the chantry chapel of the Dinhams, which includes the rather forlorn figures of John Dinham and his good lady, carved from a local lias.

Oakhill, Binegar and Leigh upon Mendip

16 miles

The countryside of East Mendip may lack the drama of Cheddar Gorge or Wookey Hole – those rugged features to be found further west in this upland region – but this is still a landscape dominated by that grey carboniferous limestone. The cottages and houses in each village, the stone walls and stiles, the church towers and pinnacles are all lovingly crafted from this solid – if forbidding – bedrock. East Mendip is very much a workaday landscape, without twee picture postcard villages. This is a region where agriculture and quarrying are still the mainstays of life in many a village community, whilst at Oakhill there is still a traditional real ale brewery. This area is not without its cultural or educational highpoints, however. At Stratton-on-the-Fosse we find the majestic Downside Abbey and its adjoining Catholic public school. This cycle tour is a fine introduction to the East Mendip countryside, exploring a good number of rugged villages as well as a sizeable chunk of its undulating – and, at times, hilly – natural landscape.

Map: OS Landranger 183 Yeovil and Frome (GR 635473).

Starting point: Oakhill's High Street. Oakhill lies on the A367 between Shepton Mallet and Radstock. Opposite the village church, which lies on the main road, turn into the High Street, where there is plenty of room for considerate roadside parking.

Refreshments: Along the way, there are pubs and hostelries in just about every village. Particularly recommended is the Vobster Inn, a delightful country pub, whilst at journey's end a pint of the locally brewed Oakhill Bitter can be enjoyed in the Oakhill Inn.

The route: Although no main roads have to be followed on this route, both the A37 and the A367 do have to be crossed on a couple of occasions. The route is also fairly hilly in places, especially south of Vobster and west of Oakhill. For every ascent, however, there is a relaxing and carefree descent!

---

1. Cycle the whole length of the High Street away from the A367 and continue for ¾ mile to reach the A37. Follow the lane opposite – it soon **bears L** – and climb uphill for ½ mile to its junction with the Old Frome Road. **Turn R**, and follow the Old Frome Road for 1½ miles to a left turn to Chilcote. Ignoring this turning, continue for another ½ mile and, on a left-hand bend, take a sharp **R turn** along an

Along the way

unmarked lane. Follow this lane up to the B3139, **turn R**, pass the Slab House Inn and continue to a junction with the B3135. **Turn R** – signposted to Shepton Mallet and Frome – and, in 200 yards, **turn L** along an unmarked side lane. Follow this narrow byway for 1½ miles to a crossroads on the edge of Binegar. **Turn R**, and follow a road that winds its way past Binegar church and on for ½ mile to the A37 in Gurney Slade.

2. **Turn R**, pass the St George Inn and take the first **L turn** signposted to Oakhill and Stratton-on-the-Fosse. Almost immediately, **turn L** again along the Stratton-on-the-Fosse turning. Follow this lane past a quarry and continue for 2 miles to its junction with the B3356. Follow the road opposite for ¾ mile down to the A367 in Stratton. **Turn L**, and then **turn R** at the second turning on the right signposted to Holcombe. In ¼ mile, **turn R** in front of Church Farm, and continue for 1½ miles to a crossroads in Holcombe, passing the Ring o' Roses Inn along the way. Cross over – waymarked to Coleford, Frome and Mells – and continue for 1 mile to a junction at Lypeate Cross. **Turn L** and, in just a few yards, **turn R** along the lane to Newbury. Follow this lane for 2 miles, ignoring all side turns, to a junction, passing Newbury House along the way.

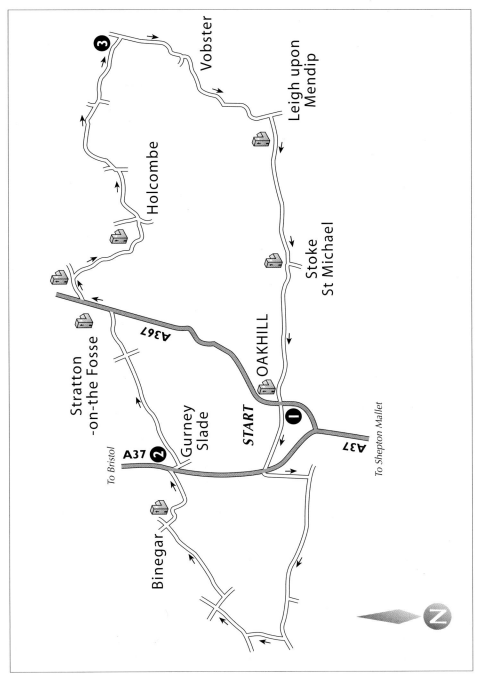

3. Turn R, and continue for ¾ mile down into Vobster. At the junction by the Vobster Inn, **turn L** along the road to Leigh upon Mendip. Follow this road for 1½ miles up to a junction on the eastern edge of Leigh, where you **turn R** to cycle through the village, passing both the church and the village inn on the way. Continue along this road for 1½ miles to a junction in Stoke St Michael. **Turn R** – waymarked to Bath – pass the Knatchbull Arms and continue for 2 miles to Oakhill. Join the A367 just past the Oakhill Inn, **turn R** and then take the first **turn L** back to the High Street.

• •

OAKHILL

Oakhill is no twee, picture-postcard village. Instead, its cottages and house are carved from the somewhat sombre grey limestone for which East Mendip is so renowned – indeed, one local author uses adjectives such as 'dour', 'sturdy' and 'characterful' in his description of the village. Oakhill is best known for its brewery, whose origins can be traced back as far as the 18th century. Its flagship ale at that time was the wonderfully named Oakhill Invalid Stout. The original brewery was destroyed by fire in 1924, and it was another 60 years before Oakhill brews began to reappear on the market. Today's brewery received long overdue recognition in 1997 when Oakhill Best Bitter won the 'Champion Beer Award' at the 'Taste of the West' competition at the nearby Bath and West Show.

STRATTON-ON-THE-FOSSE

Stratton-on-the-Fosse would rate barely a footnote in local topographic guidebooks were it not for the presence of Downside School and its magnificent abbey church. Larger than Truro cathedral, the church was built between 1870 and 1938 in a neo-Gothic style, with a tower that rises to a magnificent 166 feet. Needless to say, it dominates the surrounding landscape, serving as a landmark for many miles roundabout. The seven chapels contain collected works of art of diverse origin, including a Spanish statue of the Madonna, a copy of the statue of the Notre Dame de For from Dinant in Belgium and the 'Adoration of the Magi', a 16th-century triptych of Flemish origin. Internally, there is a significant French influence, with much rib vaulting, statuary and colourful windows.

HOLCOMBE

A former coal-mining village, Holcombe now owes much of its livelihood to quarrying and related industries. Today's settlement is largely a rambling hilly street of fairly contemporary dwellings, which has been described as 'neither exhilarating nor exactly depressing'. Oddly, Holcombe means quite literally 'the hollow or deep combe', and herein lies a clue to this village's past. The early settlement grew up around a wooded valley to the north, where today all that remains is the parish church. It is claimed that the Black Death killed off – quite literally – the first settlement, leading to a re-siting of the local community. A mound in the churchyard is said to represent a pile of the plague's victims! It is worth taking a detour to the church, not for some gruesome spectacle, but to seek out a tomb at the rear of the church. Here lie the remains of the Scott family – the mother, father, brother and sister of the Antarctic explorer.

Wedmore and Brent Knoll

16 miles

The dominant landmark in this corner of Somerset is Brent Knoll, an isolated hill that rises almost triumphantly out of the excessively horizontal landscape that stretches out between Wedmore and the Bristol Channel. Surrounded by what are the north-western fringes of the Somerset Levels, the contrast between this spectacular area of high ground and its surrounding lowlands could not be more marked. With the majority of the route crossing terrain that barely rises more than 10 feet above sea-level, to be confronted with an upland outlier that reaches over 450 feet above sea-level is an impressive sight.

Although this corner of Somerset lost much of its solitude and tranquillity with the arrival of the M5 motorway heading down to Devon from the Midlands, there is much along the way that will serve to restore that contented mien. The splendours of Wedmore church, the isolation of Mark Moor, the views from the western flanks of Brent Knoll and that final descent from Sand into the old heart of Wedmore will linger long in the memory.

Map: OS Landranger 182 Weston-super-Mare and Bridgwater (GR 435479).

Starting point: Wedmore church. Wedmore lies on the B3139 road from Wells to Burnham-on-Sea. Follow this road from the centre of Wedmore towards Burnham, and the first road you turn into is Church Street, where there is ample roadside parking alongside the magnificent parish church.

Refreshments: There are several pubs along the way, including the Wellington Arms at Rooks Bridge, the Packhorse Inn at Mark and the Brent Knoll Inn at East Brent. Back in Wedmore, just along the road from the church, is the George, a rambling old coaching inn. Do watch out, though, as you step down into the bar that lies below the level of the coachyard.

The route: Other than having to cross the busy A38 on a couple of occasions – and the need to cross the A370 on just one occasion – this route follows quiet lanes and byways across the north-western fringes of the Somerset Levels. The terrain is virtually horizontal throughout, except for one stiff climb across the western fringes of Brent Knoll. The reward, however, comes in the form of exceptional views across large tracts of this corner of Somerset, which encompass both the Bristol Channel and the Mendip Hills.

1. Take the B3139 Burnham road out of Wedmore. In ½ mile, just past Wedmore First School, **turn L** onto a side lane – there is no signpost. In 300 yards, at a T-junction, **turn R**. Continue for ¾ mile to a crossroads, and keep ahead along the road signposted to

The M5 running past Brent Knoll

Heath House and Westham. In 600 yards, having passed Walnut Tree Farm and a converted redbrick chapel, **turn R** along the lane to Westham. Follow this lane for 1¼ miles to a junction in Westham by Laurel Farm. **Turn L** and, in ½ mile, **turn R** at a junction. Follow this lane for 2 miles through to the B3139 in Mark, by the Packhorse Inn.

2. **Turn L** along the B3139 to a bend by the White Horse Inn. **Turn R** on this bend into Vole Road, and follow this lane for ½ mile to a junction by Wellfield House. Keep on the 'main' lane that **bears R** and heads northwards – bringing fine views towards the Mendip Hills – to reach the next junction in ¾ mile in Vole. Ignoring the left-turn,

follow the lane ahead for 2 miles to Rooks Bridge and the A38. Cross the main road, and follow the lane opposite, signposted to Edingworth. In ¾ mile, at a T-junction, **turn R** and follow the road up to and over the M5 before descending to the next junction. **Turn L** – signposted to Weston – and follow this road for ¼ mile to a junction by Laurel Farm. **Turn L**, and follow this lane for 1¼ miles to its junction with Brent Road by the Brent Knoll Inn.

3. Dismount, and push your cycle along the 'No entry' road to the right to reach the A370. Cross the A370, and continue along Brent Road into East Brent. Some 600 yards on from the A370, **turn L** along a side lane opposite a

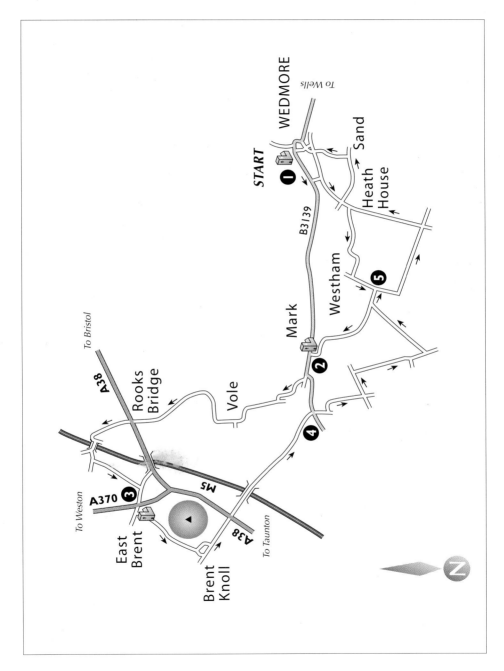

bungalow called Niagara. Follow this lane for 1¼ miles across the western flanks of Brent Knoll and down to a junction in Brent Knoll village. **Turn L** along Church Lane – passing St Michael's church – before you **bear R** down to a junction by Brent Knoll Primary School. **Turn L** and head along to the A38 – at this point a busy dual carriageway. Cross with care, and follow the lane opposite, signposted to Mark. Follow this road for 2 miles to its junction with the B3139.

4. Cross over the B3139 and follow Yardwall Road, which is signposted to Burtle, Edington and Glastonbury. Follow this lane – it **bears L** and **R** early on – for 1 mile to the next crossroads. **Turn L** – signposted to Mark and Wells – and, in ½ mile at the next junction, just beyond an aerial mast, **turn R** and follow a lane in a southerly direction for 1 mile to a junction by Mark Moor Farm. Keep ahead, crossing a drainage channel, along the road signposted to Edington and Glastonbury. In 200 yards, at the next junction, **turn L** along the road signposted to Blackford. Follow this lane for 1½ miles to reach a junction passed earlier on the route. **Turn R** – signposted to Blackford and Wedmore – and continue for ¼ mile to reach the next junction.

5. **Turn R**, and follow a lane for 1½ miles – there is an early sharp left bend – to reach a crossroads. **Turn L**, and follow a lane for 1¼ miles across the open moors – crossing the North Drain – and continue uphill to a crossroads in Heath House. **Turn R** along the road signposted to Mudgley and Theale. Follow this lane for 1 mile to a junction on the far side of the hilltop settlement of Sand. **Turn L** along the road to Wedmore, and drop downhill to a junction on the edge of Wedmore by Eglantine House. **Turn R** – signposted to Shapwick and Glastonbury – and continue to the next junction, marked by a mini-roundabout. Keep ahead into Grant's Lane and drop downhill, passing the local Baptist church on the right, to reach a junction with the B3139. **Turn L** into the Borough and, just before the Swan Inn, **turn L** into Church Street.

● ●

WEDMORE

Today Wedmore is a village of some substance, with commuters and retired well-to-do citizens having been attracted to a settlement of both quality and character. Not that this is anything new – King Alfred had a residence here and it was at Wedmore that the treaty was signed which severed the Danish hold on southern England. Overlooking the village is the imposing church, whose massive central tower dates back to Norman times and whose south doorway still has its original ironwork. Below the church lies the Borough, the main shopping area in the village. Many of the properties here have Georgian frontages, whilst the sharp-eyed visitor will spot a diminutive mullioned building of 1680 with an inscription to 'John Westover, Chyrurgeon'. The Westovers, father and son, were both surgeon members of a well-known Wedmore family.

The North Drain

BRENT KNOLL

Brent Knoll almost literally rises like an island from the surrounding levels of central Somerset. The triangulation pillar stands at the 450 feet mark, and commemorates various jubilees and coronations. The hilltop was fortified by Iron Age settlers, and their defensive ramparts are remarkably well-preserved. This tradition of defence continued right up to the last war, when trenches were excavated on the hilltop for use by the Home Guard. The Iron Age pottery fragments found on the site can be seen at the Woodspring Museum in nearby Weston-super-Mare. The outlook from this lofty hilltop – even for the cyclist merely crossing its western flanks – is quite exceptional. For those who walk to the top of Brent Knoll, Glastonbury Tor, the Quantock Hills, Exmoor, Bridgwater Bay, the Bristol Channel and the Mendip Hills are all within sight of the hilltop.

EAST BRENT

East Brent is a pretty village, with a good number of charming cottages that set off the magnificent slender spire of its church. Inside, the church can boast a good number of carved bench-ends, as well as a beautiful 17th-century plaster ceiling in the nave, which has been compared to an item of fretwork or cake-icing. It was in East Brent that the tradition of Harvest Home festivities was begun way back in 1857. These traditions continue to this day, the third Thursday in August being the busiest day in East Brent's calendar. The festivities last all day; a giant marquee is erected and the locals process through the village, led by a band, to eventually partake of a veritable feast. The length of the marquee is lined with ivy ropes, whilst hoops and banners, corn and flowers add to the colour of the scene.

8

Cannington and Steart

16 miles

The River Parrett flows into the Bristol Channel – or, more specifically, Bridgwater Bay – just to the north of the remote hamlet of Steart. This diminutive collection of cottages and farms lies a couple of miles along a cul-de-sac lane that runs the length of the Steart Peninsula, bounded to the west by the Bristol Channel and to the east by the tidal mouth of the Parrett. This is a flat and often bleak landscape, reminiscent of East Anglia or northern Holland, with big skies and open vistas.

The approach to Steart is by way of the undulating countryside that so typifies what one guidebook writer describes as 'the Quantock seaboard'. The countryside in this corner of the county can still boast a number of small-scale traditional farms that have managed to survive the competitive pressures inflicted upon them by modern agri-businesses. Along the way lies the occasional sleepy hamlet or village – such as Edbrook or Bonson, Coultings or Stockland Bristol – often little more than half-a-dozen cottages set deep in the Somerset countryside.

Map: OS Landranger 182 Weston-super-Mare and Bridgwater (GR 258394).

Starting point: The roadside by Cannington Brook in Cannington. Enter the village from the A39 bypass to the south of Cannington and, in 300 yards, fork left by a telephone box. Park on what is a loop off the main road into the village, by an ancient bridge over Cannington Brook. Across the river lies the Friendly Spirit public house.

Refreshments: At the end of the circuit, in Cannington, the route ends up by the Friendly Spirit public house, whilst a detour into Combwich takes the ride past both the Old Ship Inn and the Anchor Inn, whose names give a definite flavour of the nautical traditions of this village. If you decide to take a packed lunch, the nature reserve – with its hides – at Steart would provide a perfect place to rest and linger awhile, as would the beach just a mile south-west of Steart.

The route: The section of the route between Stockland Bristol and Steart is an absolute delight for cyclists, the only slight incline being where the lane climbs to cross a bridge over a drainage ditch! The remainder of the circuit is undulating, rather than flat, although none of the climbs could be described as anything other than moderate. The lanes and byways are generally devoid of traffic, with the possible exception of the final couple of miles between Combwich and Cannington. Fortunately, a tarmac path – seldom used by pedestrians – borders the road at this point.

The mudflats at Combwich Creek

1. Return to the main road in Cannington – the A39, before the bypass – and **turn L** to head into the village. Continue up to – and round – a sharp left-hand bend and, in 150 yards, **turn R** along the road signposted to Hinkley Point and Combwich. In 300 yards, at the top of a climb, **turn L** along an unmarked side lane. Follow this for 250 yards to a crossroads; head straight over and continue for 2¼ miles along a winding lane to a junction by a whitewashed cottage in the hamlet of Bonson. **Turn R**, and continue for ½ mile into Coultings and the next junction. Keep ahead – signposted to Stolford and Stogursey – and continue for ¾ mile to a T-junction.

2. **Turn R** – signposted to Bridgwater – and, in ½ mile, take the **L turn** signposted to Stockland and Steart. Follow this lane for 1¼ miles, passing through Stockland Bristol along the way, to a junction on a sharp right-hand bend. To visit Steart Point Reserve, **turn L** and continue in a northerly direction for 2½ miles, passing through the hamlet of Steart along the way, to a point where the lane ends at a gate. Follow the track beyond this gate for 200 yards, **turn R** and, in 75 yards, **turn L** to head up to the entrance of the Steart Point Reserve, with its hides overlooking Bridgwater Bay. Having taken time to visit the reserve, retrace the route back to the

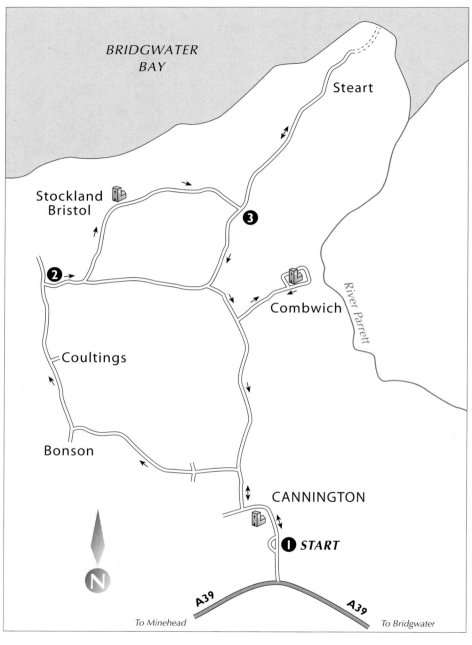

BRIDGWATER
BAY

Steart

Stockland
Bristol

2

3

Coultings

Combwich

River Parrett

Bonson

CANNINGTON

1 *START*

N

A39

A39

To Minehead

To Bridgwater

junction near Stockland Bristol to rejoin the main route.

3. At this junction, **bear** L along the road to Cannington and Bridgwater. Follow this road for 1 mile, passing through Otterhampton, to a junction. **Turn L** – signposted to Cannington and Bridgwater – and head downhill for ¾ mile before taking the **L turn** into Combwich. In ¼ mile, **keep L** into Church Hill before following the road to the right down Ship Lane, passing the Old Ship Inn. Beyond the inn, **bear R** to pass the Anchor Inn, then **bear R** past some moorings back to a junction. Follow the road ahead out of Combwich back to its junction with Cannington Road. **Turn L**, and follow this road back into Cannington, making use of the tarmac path that runs parallel to the road. At the junction with the former A39 in Cannington, **turn L** and retrace the route back to the parking area.

● ●

CANNINGTON

Although surrounded by modern housing, the centre of Cannington still manages to convey the atmosphere of a traditional rural village. Dominating the scene is the tower of St Mary's church overlooking a row of red-brick cottages, whilst nearby the Cannington Brook flows beneath an ancient packhorse bridge overlooked by lofty chestnut trees. A renowned agricultural college is based in a former priory to the north of the church. The priory was founded by Robert de Courcy in the 12th century.

STEART

Steart lies at the end of a lane that crosses flat, salty fields that eventually fade into saltmarsh and sea. What brings most visitors to Steart is the nature reserve at Steart Point, overlooking Bridgwater Bay. The coastline here is low-lying with vast mud flats exposed at low tide. This does prove to be a rather desolate spot in mid-winter when a northerly wind is blowing across the bay. The waders who flock to the area in winter make Bridgwater Bay the most important area for numbers and variety of species on the eastern shores of the Severn Estuary. Up to 10,000 dunlin are present in the bay in mid-winter, and the sight of these birds twisting and turning, particularly before roosting, is most impressive.

COMBWICH

Combwich has been described as possessing a certain 'Dutch remoteness' as it stands looking across the mud flats of the Parrett towards Pawlett Hams, with the church spire, red roofs and the masts of sailing boats combining to form a most evocative scene. The village cricket pitch, where a six could quite literally end up in the river, further complements this. In years gone by, Combwich was one of the many minor ports that made the Bristol Channel and its tributaries such a hive of activity. Along the Parrett would come vessels from South Wales laden with coal, which would then return downstream carrying dairy produce from the local farms. Salmon fishing also occurred on the Parrett, a river which Samuel Taylor Coleridge referred to as 'filthy'. In typical poetic fashion, he commented that 'it was as if all the parrots in the House of Commons had been washing their consciences in it'.

Burtle and the Polden Ridge

15 miles

This cycle tour explores what can only be described as the real heart of Somerset. Hereabouts, deep in the Somerset Levels, lie some of the most traditional farms still left in this country. This is a landscape that, were it not for a complex of drainage channels, would quite literally be under water. Artificial cuts – such as the Huntspill River and King's Sedgemoor Drain – are massive constructions, and serve as a constant reminder of how vulnerable the area is to flooding during wet winter weather. Pumping stations, like the one passed at Gold Corner, come into their own at such times.

Separating the Vale of Avalon to the north from Sedgemoor to the south is a low-lying ridge known as the Polden Hills. Although rising to little more than 300 feet in height, the contrast with the surrounding levels will certainly come as a shock to the unsuspecting cyclist! Whilst the gentle climb from Catcott onto the ridge may have you catching your breath, the subsequent freewheel down the southern slopes of the Poldens into Stowell is ample reward.

Map: OS Landranger 182 Weston-super-Mare and Bridgwater (GR 395433).

Starting point: Station Road in Burtle, by the village church. Burtle lies on an unclassified road running from the B3151 at Meare to the B3139 at Mark. Heading west through the village, having passed the local pub and shop, the next left turn is into Station Road. Park on the roadside by the church.

Refreshments: The one public house along the way – the Crown at Catcott – appears after just 3 miles of the route. This is probably far too early for a drink! A better option is to seek refreshment at journey's end in Burtle, where the Burtle Inn will no doubt be a welcome sight. There are a number of seats on the cyclepath north of Bawdrip. This would be a perfect spot to pause and enjoy a packed meal, with over half of the route having been completed.

The route: Other than a short section of the A39 between Chedzoy and Bawdrip, the rest of this cycle tour follows quiet unclassified lanes. The majority of the route crosses tracts of the Somerset Levels, with barely a gradient in sight, although the ridge formed by the Polden Hills does have to be negotiated between Catcott and Stawell. An added attraction is a cyclepath that runs between Bawdrip and Cossington. Forming part of the National Cycleway 3, this traffic-free section of the ride follows the bed of the long disused Burtle to Bridgwater railway.

The Huntspill River

1. Return to the 'main' road through Burtle, and **turn R** in the direction signposted to Westhay. Follow this road as far as the Burtle Inn, and **turn R** along the Catcott road. In 2½ miles, having passed the Crown Inn on the edge of Catcott, keep on the lane as it **bears R**, then **L**, before reaching a junction in Catcott itself by the war memorial. Follow the road directly ahead at this point, soon passing the entrance to Catcott church on the left. Keep on this road – Manor Road – as it **bears R** before reaching a road junction in front of Edington chapel. **Turn R** and, at a crossroads in 100 yards, **turn L** along the road signposted to Taunton and Bridgwater. Follow this road for ¾ mile as it climbs the northern slopes of the Polden Hills before joining the A39.

2. Follow the lane opposite – slightly to the right – signposted to Stawell and Sutton Mallet. In ½ mile, at a minor crossroads, **turn R** to Stawell. Follow this lane for 1¾ miles to reach a T-junction, passing through Stawell along the way. **Turn R**, and follow the road into Chedzoy, crossing King's Sedgemoor Drain and passing through the hamlet of Parchey en route. Some 100 yards past Chedzoy church, **turn R** along Higher Road – signposted to Bridgwater. Follow this road for 1¾ miles to the A39.

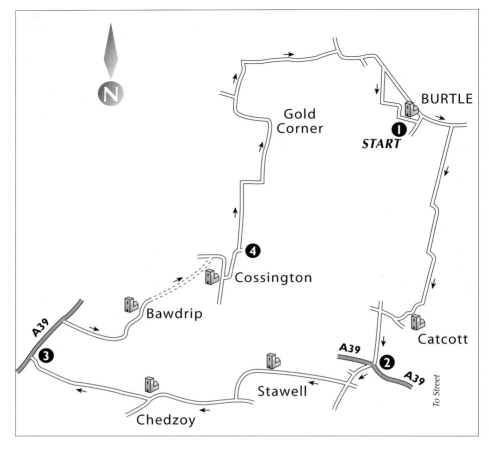

3. Turn R and, in 600 yards, **turn R** at the turning signposted to Bradney and Bawdrip. In 1½ miles, in Bawdrip, **keep R** at a fork and follow the lane up past the church, which is on your left-hand side. Just past the church, at a junction, **turn R** into a cul-de-sac lane. In 100 yards, just before the village hall and its car park, **turn L**. This is National Cycleway 3. Follow what becomes a cyclepath for ¾ mile to join a lane in Cossington. **Turn R**, and follow this lane – it soon **bears R** – down towards the church and manor in Cossington. Just before the walled manor on the right, **turn L** by a small green into a side lane. In 50 yards, at a junction, **turn L** and follow the lane out of Cossington.

4. In ¼ mile, this lane drops downhill onto the open levels, and fine views can be enjoyed towards the Mendip Hills. Keep on this lane for 1½ miles until it reaches Gold Corner, with its complex of drainage ditches and pumping station. Cross the Huntspill River and keep on the lane as it **bears L**, crossing the Cripps River. Keep on this lane for ¾ mile to the next junction. Keep ahead –signposted Edington, Burtle and Glastonbury – for 1½ miles to the next junction. Follow the road ahead at this point for ½ mile before **turning R**, ignoring an earlier right turn. This turning is not signposted and is just before the Burtle village sign. Follow this side lane for 1 mile as it winds its way around to the road junction by Burtle church.

● ●

BURTLE

Burtle lies in the heart of the Somerset Levels, an area renowned for its traditional agriculture, peat extraction and cider production. The Burtle Inn, along with most of the local pubs, was a cider house during much of the 20th century. At its peak, 25,000 gallons of cider a year were brewed hereabouts – cider with quite a reputation. In 1985, for example, Burtle cider won top prizes in the sweet, medium and dry draught categories at the Bath and West Show. Cider production occurs to this day, albeit on a much reduced scale.

CATCOTT, POLDEN HILLS, STAWELL, CHEDZOY, KING'S SEDGEMOOR DRAIN

Catcott lies in the lee of the Polden Hills, a small ridge which separates the northern levels – known as the Vale of Avalon – from Sedgemoor to the south. Catcott church is well worth a visit. The interior is renowned for its early 19th century furnishing, in particular the seating that was common at the time. On the southern sun-warmed slopes of the Polden Hills, the route passes through Stawell and Chedzoy. And it is no surprise to find fruit growing here, which may be picked in season by the public. Carving a course between Stawell and Chedzoy is King's Sedgemoor Drain, 15 feet deep, 55 feet wide at the surface and just 10 feet wide at the bottom. This drain cost £15,000 to construct, with its associated ditches and rhynes – cut to drain the surrounding fields – costing a further £28,000. In its day, this was a vast sum of money.

GOLD CORNER PUMPING STATION

This is one of the many pumps on the levels that ensures that the surrounding area does not resemble an inland sea. The diesel engines at Gold Corner are capable of shifting some 250 million gallons of water over a 24-hour period, thus ensuring that the local moors remain largely dry in winter months. Gold Corner came to the fore during the Second World War. The munitions factory at nearby Puriton needed 3.5 million gallons of water each day. A channel was constructed between the Parrett estuary and Gold Corner. Called the Huntspill River, this long thin reservoir – some five miles in length – remains an impressive sight to this day.

Glastonbury, Shapwick Heath and Westhay Moor

16 miles

To the west of the magical and mystical town of Glastonbury lie the peat moors, vast tracts of low-lying land – formerly primeval marsh – now protected from flooding by a network of drainage ditches, pumping stations and sluices. This is an open landscape with barely a hedgerow in sight, crossed by a series of long straight lanes and byways that make for perfect cycling . . . unless strong westerly winds are coming in off the Bristol Channel! The route initially heads west, towards Ashcott Corner and Shapwick Heath. This remnant of the raised bogs that once stretched to within a few miles of the coast is now a nature reserve of international importance. To the north of Shapwick, the route crosses Westhay Moor, a series of flooded peat workings, that is yet another wildfowl site of international importance. This is a fascinating cycle tour through a genuinely unique corner of the British Isles.

Map: OS Landranger 182 Weston-super-Mare and Bridgwater (GR 494396).

Starting point: Glastonbury Football Club. Follow the Glastonbury bypass to the Northload Bridge roundabout, before turning onto the B3151 Wedmore turning. In a short distance, take the right turn signposted to Godney, before turning right into the football club car park.

Refreshments: Along the way, there are inns at Ashcott Corner, Westhay and Godney, although the Peat Moors Visitor Centre near Westhay is perhaps a more interesting stop-off point. In addition to an interpretive display relating to the levels, there is also the Willows Tearoom, which serves a tempting range of meals and snacks.

The route: Other than a few busy streets in and around Glastonbury, and ¾ mile of the B3151 north of Westhay, this route follows quiet lanes, tracks and cyclepaths across the heart of the Somerset Levels. The route does include a couple of off-road sections – a two-mile track across Shapwick Heath and similar lengths of track across Westhay Moor. The occasional large lump of gravel should be avoided, although the odds on a puncture are minimal.

---

1. Leave the car park, **turn L** and cycle down to the B3151. **Turn R** and cross a river before you **turn L** along an unmarked lane. In 350 yards, by the entrance to a works complex, keep on this lane as it

A reconstructed hut at the Peat Moor Visitor Centre

bears L, then **R**, before reaching a roundabout. Keep directly ahead to reach a second roundabout, where you **turn R** into Porchestall Drove. Having passed a warehouse on the left, continue for 200 yards to an unmarked right turn. Take this **R-turn** and, in 400 yards, **turn L** by a gateway onto a recently created cyclepath. Follow this path for 600 yards to a road junction just beyond the River Brue. **Turn R**, before taking the first **L turn** along the lane signposted to Sharpham. Follow this lane for 1 mile to a junction by business premises carrying the name 'Durstons'.

2. Turn R, and follow the lane for 1¼ miles to a junction at the top of a rise, just past West Park Farm. **Turn R** and, in 250 yards, **turn R** again along an unmarked lane. Continue to the junction with the Ashcott to Meare road. **Turn R**, and continue for ¾ mile to the entrance to the Shapwick Heath Nature Reserve on the left-hand side. **Turn L**, and follow the track across Shapwick Heath for 1¼ miles to a road. **Turn R**, cycle past the Peat Moors Visitor Centre and continue for 1 mile to reach the B3151 in Westhay. Follow this occasionally busy road ahead for ½ mile to a distinct bend where a right turn is signposted to Godney.

3. Turn R at this junction, and follow the lane ahead for ½ mile, as

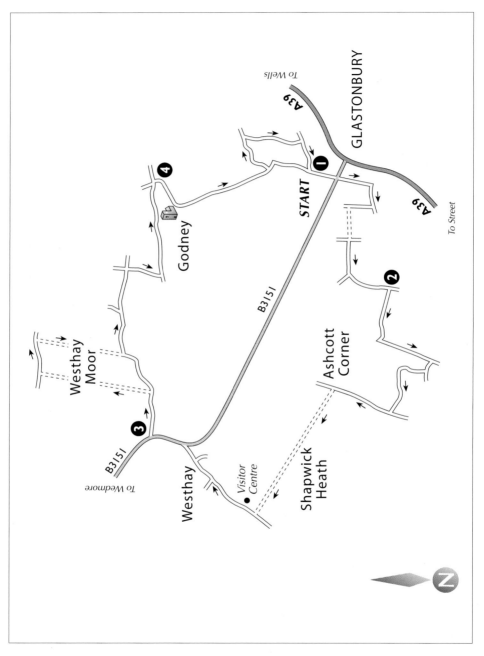

far as the second drove track on the left. **Turn L**, and follow this unmetalled track northward for 1¼ miles to a lane. **Turn R**, and continue for 500 yards to a minor crossroads. **Turn R**, and follow another drove track southwards across Westhay reserve to its junction with a lane. **Turn L**, and follow this lane for 1¼ miles to a crossroads. **Turn R** towards Godney, **bearing L** as the lane enters the village. Continue along this lane for 1¼ miles to a crossroads on the far side of Godney, passing the Sheppey Inn along the way.

4. **Turn R** – signposted to Glastonbury – and follow this lane in a southerly direction for 1½ miles to a point, just beyond a bridge, where a side lane goes off on the left. **Turn L** at this point, and follow the lane ahead – Great Withy Drove – to a junction in ½ mile. **Turn R** – the OS map labels this lane Black Pit Drove – to a junction just past Common Moor Farm. **Turn R**, and continue to a junction by Sweetacre Nursery. **Turn L**, and the first **L turn** returns this cycle tour to the car park.

● ● ● ● ● ● ● ● ● ● ● ● ● ● ● ● ● ● ● ●

GLASTONBURY

Glastonbury is a place of legend. The Glastonbury thorn that grows on Wearyall Hill and in the abbey grounds, allegedly sprouted from the staff of Joseph of Arimathea, visiting Britain after the Crucifixion; the waters of the Chalice Well flow red because Joseph is said to have deposited the Chalice Cup of the Last Supper beneath its waters . . . although the presence of local iron deposits may just be nearer the truth! The bodies of King Arthur and Queen Guinevere are said to repose in the abbey grounds, with the site of the tomb still commemorated with a plaque, whilst the tor was supposedly the entrance to the underworld, the kingdom of Annwn. Certainly, the town acts as a magnet to any number of travelling folk whose beards, beads and balding pates dominate the high street!

SHAPWICK HEATH

Shapwick Heath contains remnants of the raised bogs that once ran to within a few miles of the Somerset coast. A wide range of vegetation types is to be found on the heath, from poor fen and bog myrtle pastures through to birch and alder. The most obvious land use, however, is peat extraction, with vast tracts of the heath looking for all intents and purposes like areas of opencast mining. The area is perhaps best known for its rich butterfly and dragonfly population, whilst it is not unknown for roe deer to be seen in the thickets.

WESTHAY

Westhay is a small village consisting largely of scattered farms. One of the local farmers, Mr Ray Sweet, was clearing the ditches on his land in 1970, when he stumbled across pieces of waterlogged timber and a flint arrowhead. Expert archaeological advice was summoned and an ancient trackway discovered. Subsequently named the Sweet Track, this routeway, which dates from 4000 BC, is believed to be the world's oldest footpath. Basically, what Ray Sweet had discovered was the remains of a gangway constructed of wooden poles, which enabled ancient fishermen and hunters to make their way across what was then a waterlogged landscape. The Willows Garden Centre, which is passed along the way, houses the Peat Moors Visitor Centre. As well as displays relating to the local peat industry, a mock-up section of the Sweet Way can be seen.

WESTHAY MOOR

Westhay Moor was described in the Middle Ages as being 'wet and weely, miry and moorish'. This is a rather gloomy picture for a landscape that has more recently been described as 'wild country . . . fascinating and quite magical'. The second description is far closer to the truth! This damp, low-lying peat moor is criss-crossed by a network of drainage ditches, known as 'rhynes'. This watery environment provides a natural home for such diverse wildfowl as swans, herons and kingfishers, whilst flocks of peewits are a common sight in the surrounding fields. Part of the exhausted peat working has been purchased by the Somerset Trust for Nature Conservation and is being developed as the Greater Westhay Reserve. Alder and willow have been planted, and extensive reed beds

The cyclepath near Glastonbury

developed. The reserve has attracted badgers and foxes, kestrels and coots, as well as large numbers of dragonfly.

11

Street and Baltonsborough

15 miles

I n other parts of Britain, moorland is associated with bleak and exposed upland. Dartmoor and Exmoor spring to mind, for example. In Somerset, however, the opposite is in fact the case. The moors are the flat central region of the county, where the landscape barely rises above sea-level. This was historically boggy marsh, covered by sea at times of high tide.

This cycle tour explores Butt Moor and South Moor, as well as the rather more undulating landscape that lies to the south of these lowland areas. Along the way are the villages of Butleigh and Baltonsborough, each with an historical tale or two to tell, whilst at journey's end in Street, we find the birthplace of Clarks Shoes. Tradition goes back a long way in this corner of the county.

Map: OS Landranger 182 Weston-super-Mare and Bridgwater (GR 482365).

Starting point: Northside car park in Street. From the A39 Street bypass, follow the signs for the town centre car parking. This will take you via Farm Road into the car park.

Refreshments: There are public houses along the way at Butleigh, Barton St David and Baltonsborough, whilst at journey's end in Street you will find cafes, teashops, pubs and restaurants. The development of Clarks Village, a retail park housed in former shoe factories, has placed Street very much on the tourist trail. Perhaps the ideal place to rest and linger awhile is the Greyhound Inn at Baltonsborough, conveniently located well beyond the halfway point on the route.

The route: Other than the busy roads in Street itself, this cycle tour follows unclassified roads across a swathe of central Somerset's pastoral landscape. The outward leg of the route to Barton St David crosses an undulating landscape, with only the occasional gentle incline to test those leg muscles. Beyond Barton St David, it is level Somerset moorland all the way back into Street.

---

1. Cycle up to the supermarket at the top of the car park and **bear L** to reach Farm Road. **Turn R**, and cycle up Farm Road to its junction with the High Street. Cross over, and follow Leigh Road alongside Crispin Hall before taking the first **L turn** into Hindhayes Road. At the next minor crossroads, **turn R** into Elmhurst Lane and continue up to a set of traffic lights. Cross over into Butleigh Road, and follow this occasionally busy unclassified road out of Street, passing Millfield School along the way. In 1½ miles, at a minor crossroads, **turn R** into

The River Brue

Butleigh Wotton, cycling along Wotton Street. Continue through this hamlet for ½ mile, then just past a thatched property on the left, **turn L** along an unmarked side lane. In 1½ miles, at a minor crossroads, **turn L** into another unmarked lane and continue for ½ mile to a crossroads in Butleigh.

2. Cross over into the High Street – signposted to Baltonsborough and West Pennard – and follow this road for 300 yards before taking a **R turn** into Chapel Lane (NB: a detour to the left on this stretch of the route will bring you to St Leonard's church). Follow Chapel Lane to the next junction – opposite Dovedale Cottage – and **turn L**, before cycling up to a

crossroads by the Rose and Portcullis Inn. **Turn L** at this point, and follow the lane ahead for 2 miles to a crossroads in Barton St David, just past the Barton Inn. **Turn L** along the road signposted to Baltonsborough. Follow this road for 1½ miles into the hamlet of Catsham, before taking the second **R turn**, signposted to West Pennard. Continue for 1 mile to a junction in Ham Street, **turn R**, then **turn L** into Teapot Lane. Follow this quiet byway for ½ mile to the next junction, **turn L** and continue for ¾ mile to the next junction. **Turn L** towards West Pennard and Glastonbury and, in ½ mile, **turn L** along the road to Baltonsborough. Follow this lane for just 100 yards to a junction.

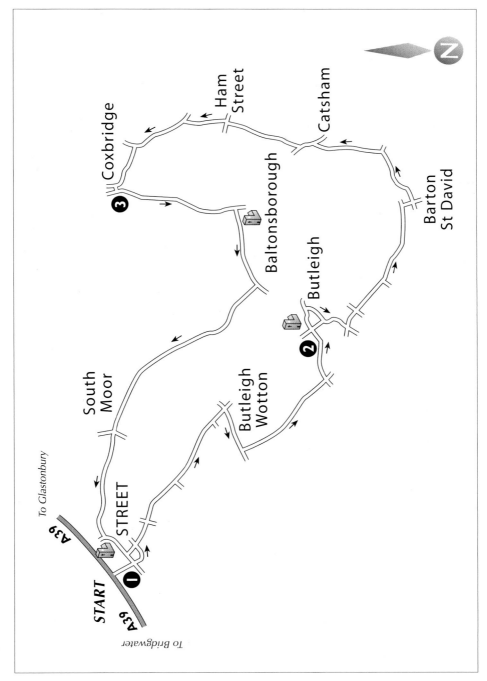

3. Turn L, and follow the road ahead for 1¼ miles into Baltonsborough. **Turn R** in front of the Greyhound Inn into Church Lane – signposted to Butleigh and Street – and follow this road for 1¼ miles to a **R turn** to Glastonbury and Street, crossing the River Brue along the way. Follow this right turn across South Moor. In 2½ miles, at a crossroads, cross over and continue for 1 mile into Street. At the first mini-roundabout, **turn L** and follow the road between Strode College on the left and a church on the right. At the next roundabout, with the Street Inn on the left, head across into the High Street before taking a **R turn** by Crispin Hall back into Farm Road and the car park.

● ●

STREET

It is the Clark family, devout Quakers, to whom Street can attribute its prosperity. The first Clark shoe factory in the town was established in 1829 as a venture between Cyrus Clark and his brother James. Amongst their earliest successes were slippers fashioned from local sheepskins. The original shoe factory today houses the Shoe Museum, which traces the development of the shoe from the Roman sandal through to the present day. Included amongst the exhibits are those classic platform shoes from the 1970s that, in retrospect, created some of the most embarrassing wedding photographs when viewed through the eyes of later generations! Shoe production in Street is sadly no more, Clark Shoes having fallen victim to changes in fashions as well as cheap imports. The many former production units now house the Clarks Village Retail Park which, fortunately for the economy of the town, attracts visitors from far and wide.

BUTLEIGH

Butleigh, located strategically above the River Brue and its floodplain, is a typical Somerset village. Hidden away off the main street is St Leonard's church, where we find monuments which pay tribute to Samuel, Arthur and Alexander Hood. Samuel – Admiral Viscount Hood, to give him his full title – was described by none other than Nelson as 'the best officer that England has to boast of'. Overlooking the churchyard is Butleigh Court, lined with graceful cedars. The Court was built as recently as 1845 in the Tudor style, and a tidy monument to that period it is too, described as 'a medley of sky-defying pepperpot chimneys, florid oriel windows, battlements, turrets and lacy traceries'. If any film producer is looking for the perfect setting for a horror movie, then look no further!

BALTONSBOROUGH

Baltonsborough – or, more correctly, the neighbouring hamlet of Ham Street – was the birthplace of St Dunstan way back in the 10th century. By 940 AD, Dunstan had risen to the heights of Abbot of Glastonbury, and just 19 years later he had attained the venerable rank of Archbishop of Canterbury. Tootle Bridge, to the south of the village, is a site of some intrigue. The bowl on its southern supports is reputedly a built-in font, believed to be the very spot where Dunstan himself was christened. A more touching tale, however, relates to a drunk who 'overspilled himself' from the bridge one dark night in the 19th century. He landed upside down in the font, his head firmly wedged under the holy waters, and was found dead the following morning!

Burrowbridge and Bridgwater

16 miles

Without doubt, the Somerset Levels provide some of the best cycling terrain not only in Somerset but also in the country. The landscape is flat throughout – although far from featureless – and is home to any number of moisture-loving plants and wildfowl, who make their home amongst the willow-lined rhynes. These drainage ditches, and the associated pumping stations, are a constant reminder that in days gone by the levels were little more than a vast inland marsh.

From Burrowbridge, whose ruinous church atop a small knoll surely deserves the same degree of recognition as Glastonbury Tor, this cycle tour follows a quiet corner of the levels through to the bustling heart of Bridgwater. A section of the Bridgwater and Taunton Canal is followed out of the town, before quiet lanes and byways – often bordered by the River Parrett – return the route to Burrowbridge. With the complete absence of contour lines along the way, this really is cycling made easy!

Map: OS Landranger 182 Weston-super-Mare and Bridgwater (GR 360306).

Starting point: Burrow Mump car park. Burrowbridge lies on the A361 between Glastonbury and Taunton. Just east of the village centre, in the shadow of the National Trust's Burrow Mump, is a car park for visitors to this little knoll crowned by a fine ruinous church.

Refreshments: Alongside the Bridgwater and Taunton Canal on the fringes of Bridgwater lies the Boat and Anchor Inn, a perfect waterside resting spot at the halfway point on the route. Beyond the Boat and Anchor, the route passes the Thatchers Arms in Moorlands – a real country pub – as well as the King Arthur Inn at journey's end. A pleasant alternative is to enjoy a picnic atop Burrow Mump at the end of a pleasant few hours cycling in the Somerset countryside.

The route: The major part of this route follows quiet lanes and byways between Burrowbridge and Bridgwater. The only section of the route where real caution needs to be exercised is in Bridgwater itself, where ½ mile of traffic-laden town centre streets are followed. If you do not feel confident cycling in town centres, you may feel happier walking this part of the tour.

---

1. Leave the car park, **turn L** and follow the A361 into Burrowbridge. Immediately before the River Parrett – and opposite the King Arthur Inn – **turn R** along a side lane. Follow this lane for 1½ miles

The view from Burrow Mump

to a junction just before Hoopers Elm Farm. Keep on the 'main' lane at this point, which **bears L** to pass the farm, ignoring the 'no through road' that lies straight ahead. In 1 mile, at the next junction, keep on the 'main' lane, which **bears R** towards Westonzoyland. In 600 yards, follow the **L turn** signposted to Andersea. Follow this lane for 1 mile to its junction with the A372, ignoring a left turn along the way into Andersea itself.

2. **Turn L**, and follow the main road for ½ mile before you **turn L** to Dunwear. Follow this road for 1 mile into Dunwear and, by the telephone box opposite Riverside House, **fork L** onto a cycle path by the River

Parrett. Follow this cycle path for 1¼ miles – passing under the M5 and a low railway bridge along the way – to some steps where the cycle path joins Salmon Parade. Follow the cycle lane ahead to the traffic lights and a junction with the A38. Cross over, and continue along Salmon Parade to its junction with Eastover alongside Town Bridge. Head straight over into East Quay and, at the next junction, by a bus depot, **turn L**. At the next junction, **turn L** and cross Chandos Bridge. Continue to some traffic lights, and **turn R** along Northgate down to Bridgwater Docks. Cross the bridge over the entrance to the docks, then **turn L** into the marina just before Russell Place.

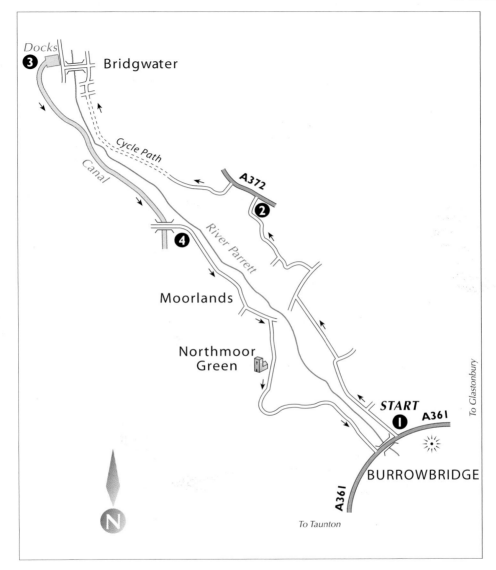

3. Follow the quayside ahead before joining the towpath of the Taunton and Bridgwater Canal, which heads out of the dock. Follow the towpath for 2 miles to a swingbridge some 300 yards before the M5 motorway. Keep ahead at this point along a tarmac lane; pass under the M5 and cross the next swingbridge on the left to rejoin the towpath by the Boat and Anchor Inn. Follow the towpath for ½ mile, before taking the path that slopes uphill from the canal to join a lane at Huntworth Bridge.

4. Turn L, cross a railway and follow the lane ahead for 1¼ miles to the Thatchers Arms in Moorlands. Continue following the 'main' lane towards Burrowbridge, passing the church of St Peter and St John in Northmoor Green in 1 mile. Continue for another 2¼ miles to the A361 in Burrowbridge, ignoring all side turnings. **Turn L**, cross the River Parrett and follow the main road back to the car park.

● ●

BURROW MUMP

Burrow Mump overshadows Burrow-bridge, a small village that straddles the A361 on its way across the levels to Taunton. This diminutive hillock, a mere 75 feet in height, would have been a small island back in the 9th century, when the local moors were little more than inland marshes. The Mump was a lookout post in those distant times, standing guard over the River Parrett and the approaches to King Alfred's headquarters at nearby Athelney. The ruined chapel at the summit of the Mump is dedicated to St Michael. Excavations have revealed earlier buildings on the site, including a Norman building that may have been a castle.

BRIDGWATER

Bridgwater is an old-established port, located downstream from where the tidal River Parrett enters the Bristol Channel. Although a rather industrialised town for Somerset, many fine old buildings still survive, including the medieval church with its tall spire, the Market Hall of 1834, the Lions – a quayside house of 1730 – and the early Georgian houses in Castle Street, used in the filming of 'Tom Jones'. The area around the docks will certainly catch the eye of any industrial archaeologists. This is a location that no doubt inspired Cromwell's Admiral Blake, one of Bridgwater's greatest sons. A statue to the admiral stands in the centre of the town, whilst the Admiral Blake Museum is located in his actual birthplace.

THE BRIDGWATER AND TAUNTON CANAL

The traditional route for waterborne vessels running from Bridgwater to Taunton was to take the navigable River Parrett upstream to Burrowbridge before heading south along the River Tone into Taunton. The route was somewhat circuitous – as well as being tidal – so it came as no surprise that during the period of canal mania in the 18th century, an artificial cut was constructed between the two towns. Opened in 1827, the Bridgwater and Taunton Canal carried 79,000 tons of cargo – mainly Welsh coal – in its heyday in 1847. At one time, the canal was part of a proposed scheme to link the Bristol Channel with the English Channel, a scheme that never came to fruition. The story of the canal's decline is the familiar one of competition from the railways, in this case Brunel's Bristol and Exeter Railway that ran between Bridgwater and Taunton. Today, the Bridgwater and Taunton Canal is fully restored, and is used by many pleasure craft navigating their way between these Somerset towns.

Castle Cary, Ditcheat and Lydford

17 miles

Much of the countryside in South Somerset makes for perfect cycling terrain. Whilst the landscape may lack the 'excessively horizontal' qualities of the Somerset Levels, the gradual ups-and-downs do bring their rewards. Barely a mile passes on this cycle tour without a gentle elevation that brings a far-ranging outlook across this quiet corner of Somerset.

Along the way lie a number of off-the-beaten-track villages and hamlets, scattered around ragged, wandering lanes that cross a landscape of pasture land, arable and orchards. Whilst few of the settlements would be described as picturesque or picture-postcard, each has an element of intrigue or surprise that will catch the eye. It is that sort of circuit – nothing to set the blood fizzing, no great dramatic points, but simply a very pleasant cycle ride.

Map: OS Landranger 183 Yeovil and Frome (GR 635335).

Starting point: Castle Cary station. The station lies alongside the A371, between Shepton Mallet and Wincanton, on the north-west fringes of the town. Park in the station car park – fee payable.

Refreshments: At journey's end, it is worth visiting Castle Cary itself – the town centre lying just 1 mile southwest of the station – if only to discover the George Inn. A lovely thatched coaching inn, the cosy beamed front bar has a massive black elm mantlebeam over the log fire, that is said to be over 1,000 years old. An alternative if you are looking for refreshment is the Brook House Inn, which lies on the A371, just to the north of the station.

The route: Other than the briefest of encounters along the way with the A37, and a short stretch of the A371 at the start of the ride, this route follows quiet lanes and byways to the west of Castle Cary. There are occasional undulations en route, but the inclines are gentle and should be within the capabilities of the majority of cyclists.

1. Leave the station car park, **turn R** along the A371 and, in 600 yards, **turn L** in front of the Brook House Inn along the road signposted to Alhampton. Follow this road northward and, in ½ mile, keep on this lane as it **bears L** into Alhampton itself. Continue along to the Alhampton Inn on the left and, just beyond this point, keep on the 'main' road as it **bears R** towards Ditcheat (signposted).

The church at West Lydford

Cross the River Alham and continue northwards for 1 mile to a T-junction in Ditcheat. **Turn L** and continue along to the post office before you **bear R**, past the Manor House Inn and the church, on the road signposted to Glastonbury. Ignoring all side turns, follow this road as it winds its way through Ditcheat before continuing for 1½ miles to its junction with the A37 in Wraxall, by the Queens Arms.

2. Cross the A37 and follow the lane opposite, signposted to West Pennard and Glastonbury. Follow this lane for 2 miles to a crossroads just past Withial Farm. At this point, **turn L** along the lane signposted to Parbrook and Lottisham. In ½ mile, at a T-junction in Parbrook, **turn L** along the road signposted to Lottisham and West Lydford, ignoring an immediate left turn to Stone. In 1 mile, pass Lottisham church on the left and, in 600 yards, **turn R** along the side turning to Southwood and West Lydford. Head south for 1½ miles to a T-junction, **turn R** – signposted to West Lydford – and follow this lane for ¾ mile to its junction with the A37 just past West Lydford village.

3. Turn L and, in 200 yards, opposite a bungalow, **turn R** into West Lane. Follow this lane into East Lydford and, in 600 yards, keep on the lane as it **bears R** to

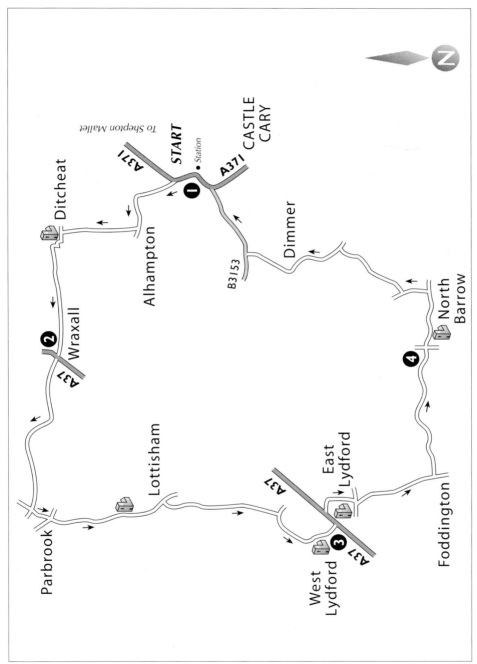

continue through the village before reaching the B3153. **Turn R** onto the B3153 and, in a few yards, **turn L** along the lane signposted to Foddington. Pass under a railway bridge, and continue for 1 mile to a junction in Foddington by Shells Farm. **Turn L** – signposted to North Barrow and Castle Cary – and follow this lane for 1½ miles to a crossroads on the edge of North Barrow.

4. Cross over into North Barrow. In ¾ mile, just before the lane climbs to cross a railway, **turn L** along an unmarked side turning. Follow this road for 1¼ miles to a T-junction by a railway bridge, keeping right early on where a drive ahead leads into Higher Thorn Farm. **Turn L** at the T-junction and follow a lane for 1¼ miles through Dimmer and on to a junction with the B3153. **Turn R**, and cycle through Clanville for ½ mile to a junction with the A371. Keep ahead for 200 yards down the main road to return to Castle Cary station.

● ●

CASTLE CARY

Castle Cary is a typical busy market town, centred upon a long main street with its 19th-century market hall. This market hall is a mixture of classical styles with columns and Jacobean windows. The town's castle is now little more than a ruin, following two sieges during the Civil War. A few remnants of the keep foundations, now an overgrown earthwork, are all that remain of the former fortification. In the town's Castle Square – actually a triangle – stands the Round House, one of the finest examples of a lock-up in the country; it was built in 1779 at a cost of £23.

DITCHEAT

The name 'Ditch-eat' is not based upon some local gastronomical defect, rather it comes from 'Dike-gate', perhaps a reference to a nearby lock-gate that historically regulated the threat of rising water levels in nearby streams and rivers. The village church has been described as 'almost awe-inspiring in its cathedral-like dimensions'. Alongside the church stands the local manor house, its gables appearing to peep over the boundary of the churchyard as if shy of being associated with its more illustrious neighbour. This long, two-storeyed building, with the aforementioned gables, bears the date 1603. The entrance hall has a window bearing the arms and crest of Dawes, a Dorset family, who acquired the manor from Lord Hopton in 1669.

WEST and EAST LYDFORD

West Lydford has a 17th-century bridge over the River Brue, five arched, with a pierced parapet to carry any flood overflow. The church, a largely Victorian reconstruction, enjoys a striking location alongside the Brue. This most photogenic of settings will have most visitors reaching for their cameras. Pevsner commented on 'the antiquarian exactitude of the reconstruction', a feature found only in structures commenced after 1840. In nearby East Lydford, the church of 1866 is by the same architect, but has a tower and spire rising to 90 feet. The guidebooks point out an alabaster relief of St George assailing a dragon, which provides a 'pleasant, if conventional, decoration'.

Williton and the Quantock Hills

19 miles

Anyone who is familiar with the film *The Land Girls* will immediately identify with the sites and locations on this particular Somerset cycle tour with the scene at Crowcombe station on the West Somerset Railway bringing about a sense of *déjà vu*. It is indeed the spot where our heroines disembarked upon their arrival in the West Country.

The circuit itself starts near the Bristol Channel coast at Williton, before heading inland to explore the lower slopes of the Quantock Hills. The views throughout are quite exceptional as the route passes from one red sandstone village to another, with the occasional cool stretch of woodland providing welcome respite along what is at times a strenuous cycle tour. An added attraction is the occasional appearance of the aforementioned West Somerset Railway, providing a nostalgic reminder of the heyday of steam in this country. It is altogether a perfect introduction to this most beautiful corner of the county, which lies 'twixt the Quantock and Brendon Hills.

Map: OS Landranger 181 Minehead and Brendon Hills (GR 078410).

Starting point: The signposted public car park that lies just off of the A39 in the centre of Williton. This is just north of the Egremont Hotel. Williton itself lies on the A39, just 8 miles east of Minehead.

Refreshments: Along the way, there are public houses in Williton, Bicknoller, Crowcombe and Stogumber. My favourite resting-place, however, is the Blue Bell in the remote hamlet of Triscombe. Tucked away in a fold in the Quantock Hills, this delightful hostelry offers imaginative food, with particular emphasis on fresh fish dishes. It is also conveniently placed at the halfway point on the route, with the more difficult hill work left behind.

The route: Much of this circuit follows quiet lanes and byways in a secluded backwater of West Somerset. The roads in and around Williton are busy, however, and due care should be taken when crossing the A358 and the A39. There are a number of hills to negotiate, the main ascents being the climb out of Doniford up to the A39, and a rather harsh ascent out of Crowcombe en route to Triscombe. The rewards for these climbs, however, are not only a series of fine views but also a number of exhilarating downhill stretches.

---

1. Leave the car park, **turn R** along the A39 and, in 50 yards, keep ahead at a junction along the B3191 signposted to Watchet. In

Crowcombe Heathfield station

150 yards, where the B3191 bears left by the Masons Arms, keep ahead past the Masons Arms, and follow this road for 1½ miles to a junction in Donniford. **Turn R** to follow the road signposted to Bridgwater for 1½ miles uphill to the A39. Cross this busy road, and follow the lane opposite signposted to Bicknoller. In 600 yards, at a crossroads, take the **R turn**, still signposted to Bicknoller. In 1 mile, **turn L** off the 'main' road along the side turn into Bicknoller itself. In ½ mile, at a crossroads in the village by the post office, keep ahead along the road signposted to Chilcombe Lane. **Turn R** into Church Lane in just 75 yards, and continue past the church and inn down to the A358.

2. **Turn L** onto the A358 – signposted to Taunton – and, in 80 yards, take the **R turn** signposted to Newton and Kingswood. In ½ mile, at a junction, follow the lane ahead to Culverhayes. In another ½ mile, at the next junction, take the **R fork** to Stogumber and continue for another ½ mile to the next junction; **turn L** along the road waymarked to Crowcombe and Bishops Lydeard. Follow this byway for 1½ miles to the A358. Cross over and follow the lane opposite into Crowcombe. Continue past the village pub and the church before taking a **L turn** towards Nether Stowey. Soon, take the **R turn** signposted to Triscombe and follow this winding and occasionally hilly lane for 1¼ miles to a junction by the Blue Ball Inn in Triscombe. **Turn R**, and follow the road downhill for 1 mile to the A358.

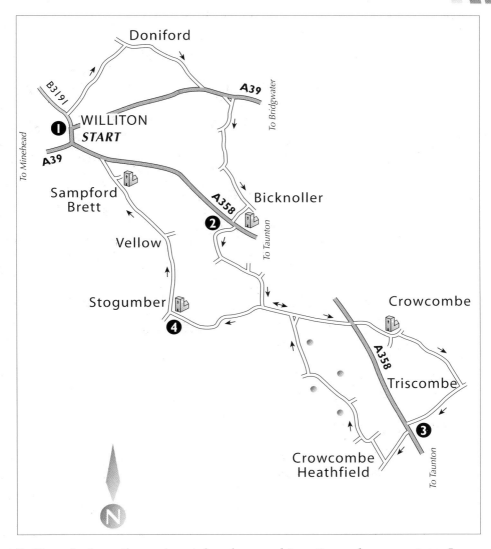

3. Turn L along the main road and, almost immediately, **turn R** along the lane signposted to Crowcombe station. In ¾ mile, just before a railway bridge, **turn R** along the access road that leads to Crowcombe station. Continue past the station buildings and on to a road junction, where you **turn L**. Cross the railway, and keep on the lane as it **bears R**. Continue along this lane, ignoring all side turns and following the signs to Heddon Oak and Stogumber. In 2 miles, on reaching the forked junction at Heddon Oak, take the **L fork** up to an immediate junction and **turn L** to follow the lane towards Stogumber. In ¾ mile, pass under the West Somerset Railway by Stogumber station before continuing for another ¾ mile into the village of Stogumber itself, to reach a T-junction in the village.

4. Turn R – signposted to Vellow and Williton – and continue for 1¼ miles into Vellow. Where the 'main' road bears right, **keep L** along a side lane to Sampford Brett. Follow this lane for 1¼ miles to a junction in Sampford Brett where the 'main' road once again bears right. At this point, keep on the side lane ahead, signposted to Williton. Follow this lane up to the A358, **turn L** and continue into Williton. At the roundabout by the Egremont Hotel, **keep R** along the A39 towards Bridgwater. A **R turn** in just 50 yards leads into the car park.

• •

WILLITON

Williton is a somewhat busy place, being at the junction of the A358 with the A39. This meeting place of main roads that radiate out to Minehead, Taunton and Bridgwater is overlooked by the Egremont Hotel, a 15th-century coaching inn. St Peter's church, on a site used for Christian worship since Saxon times, is worth seeking out, as is the unique Bakelite Museum where the exhibits show the large range of uses to which this precursor of plastic were put. Williton station, was opened in 1862 and the signal box is the last working example of those built by the Bristol and Exeter Railway.

BICKNOLLER

Bicknoller is best known for its post – the ancient boundary post of the parish, high above the village on the Quantock hilltops that acts as a landmark for walkers. The village below is typical of so many in the Quantock region, with red sandstone cottages surrounding a red sandstone church. Although there is some evidence of Norman work in the church, most of what stands is Perpendicular in design.

THE WEST SOMERSET RAILWAY

This railway recaptures the age of the branch line in the days of steam. From Bishops Lydeard, the restored locomotives run beside the Quantock Hills northwards to the Bristol Channel coast at Watchet and Blue Anchor, before heading west to the terminus in the holiday town of Minehead. Everything along its 20 mile length has been reconstructed down to the last detail, including traditional leather suitcases on the station platforms and old fashioned station flower beds.

STOGUMBER

Stogumber may be just another sleepy backwater, but it was not always this way. During the 15th and 16th centuries, the village prospered as a collection point for wool, with an open-sided market house used for fleece trading. The local merchants would distribute wool to nearby cottages, where the weaving and spinning took place, before the various products were carried on packhorse over the Quantock Hills to the River Parrett at Combwich, and then shipped to Bristol.

Nether Stowey and Lilstock

15 miles

West Somerset is associated with sleepy little villages lying along winding country lanes, set amongst a landscape of gently rolling hills and undulating countryside. This cycle tour sets out to explore a quiet corner of this part of the county, where place names such as Nether Stowey and Stogursey have a real West Country sound and feel.

As well as off-the-beaten-track villages and hamlets, there is the opportunity to visit the Bristol Channel coast just north of Lilstock. This is a little explored section of coastline, with pebbly beaches and the occasional crumbling rock face. On clear fine days, the views across the channel towards the distant Welsh Hills will be sure to impress. When the weather is overcast and grey, however, it is easy to see why this is a seldom-visited part of Britain's coastal heritage!

Maps: OS Landranger 181 Minehead and OS Landranger 182 Weston-super-Mare and Bridgwater are both needed for this cycle tour. (GR 191397).

Starting point: The Library and Quantock Office car park in Nether Stowey. From Nether Stowey's main street, turn into Castle Street. In 100 yards, a right-turn leads into the car park.

Refreshments: Pubs and inns are few and far between along the way, although the Shurton Inn at Shurton will provide welcome rest and refreshment, with the hills around Kilton and Lilstock but a distant memory. At journey's end, there are several traditional hostelries in Nether Stowey, including the Ancient Mariner and the Rose and Crown. Whichever inn takes your fancy, you can be sure that the local farm cider will prove most palatable!

The route: Other than a couple of brief encounters with the A39, this route follows a network of quiet lanes and byways across the West Somerset countryside. The only section of unmetalled road is the brief detour to visit the coastline at Lilstock. The going is undulating – rather than flat – with one or two not inconsiderable gradients in and around Kilton and Lilstock.

1. Leave the car park, **turn L** and, at the junction with the main street in Nether Stowey, **turn L** again to follow the road marked to Williton and Minehead. Follow this road past Coleridge's Cottage and the Ancient Mariner Inn up to the A39. **Turn L** and, in 150 yards, take the **R turn** signposted to Stringston. Follow this lane for 1 mile to the next junction, before taking the **R turn** (still signposted

Stogursey Castle

to Stringston). Follow this lane, ignoring all side turns, to the junction on the far side of Stringston. **Turn L** – signposted to Holford and Williton – and continue for 1¼ miles to the next T-junction. **Turn R** – waymarked to Kilton and Lilstock. In 1 mile, having passed West Kilton Farm, keep on the lane as it **bears R** and, in 150 yards, at a junction, **keep L** to pass St Nicholas' church. Follow the lane ahead for ½ mile into Lilstock, passing St Michael's church on the right as you enter this hamlet.

2. Beyond the church, keep on the lane as it **bears R** and drops downhill to Lilstock Farm. At the bend beyond this farm, a detour along the track to the left will bring you to Lilstock beach and the Bristol Channel. For the main route, follow the lane to the right and on up Cross Elms Hill to a junction in 1 mile. **Turn L** – marked to Burton and Stogursey – and continue for 1 mile to a junction in Burton by a blacksmith's. Follow the road ahead to Shurton and the Shurton Inn, before continuing for 600 yards to the next junction. **Turn R** – signposted to Combwich and Bridgwater – and follow the road for ½ mile to the next junction. **Turn R** – signposted Farringdon Lane – and head south for 1 mile to the next junction; there **turn R** and follow the road into Stogursey.

3. Just past the church, **turn L** into Castle Street – detour along a footpath to visit the castle – and continue for 1 mile to a junction just past a farm. **Turn R** – signposted Fiddington – and follow the lane ahead for 1 mile into Fiddington. Head up out of the

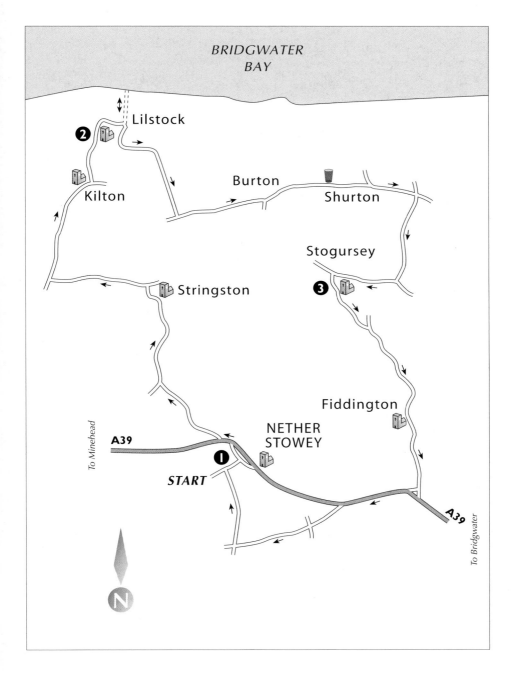

village for ½ mile to the next junction, and **turn R** to pass the Old Forge before joining the A39. **Turn R** and follow the main road for ½ mile to the Cottage Inn. Just beyond the inn, where the A39 bears right, keep ahead along a side lane to Over Stowey. In ½ mile, keep ahead at a minor crossroads and continue for a further mile to the next crossroads. **Turn R**, and follow the road for 1 mile into Nether Stowey and a junction with Castle Street. **Turn R**, then **L**, back into the car park.

NETHER STOWEY

Established around a Norman motte-and-bailey castle, Nether Stowey was built on an imposing hillock to the south of the village. Today's village is centred upon the Jubilee Clock of 1897, which stands at the junction of Castle Street with the High Street. A little brook flows the length of Castle Street, and was described by Coleridge as 'the dear gutter of Stowey'. It is in fact Coleridge – or rather his cottage standing opposite the Ancient Mariner Inn, – which attracts most visitors to Nether Stowey. Coleridge resided in Stowey between 1796 and 1798 and some of his best work was composed here, notably *The Rime of the Ancient Mariner*.

STOGURSEY

Stogursey has been described as being 'not pretty in the flowerbox sense but exuding a certain robust charm'. This outlook is especially fine, with cob and thatched cottages standing cheek by jowl with brick and stone shops on a tree-lined market space. To the south of the village lie the sparse remains of a once-proud castle, a victim of the Wars of the Roses, whilst overshadowing the centre of the village is the former priory church of St Andrew, whose leaded spire juts somewhat incongruously out of a heavy square tower. St Andrew's was originally part of a Benedictine Priory that was subservient to Lanlay in Normandy. A French family named de Curcy founded the priory church here in the 12th century – hence the village's earlier name of 'Stok Curcy'. The local villagers evidently had problems with their pronunciation, eventually deciding that 'Stogursey' was less of a mouthful! It is certainly more suited to the local burr.

KILTON and LILSTOCK

Kilton is little more than a farming hamlet, where even Pevsner was hard pushed to find much to describe. Of the one building of note he wrote just a few brief words: 'St Nicholas 1862 by John Norton incorporating Perp. Bits.' The church may be plain and functional, but its beauty lies in its pure simplicity. Over the vestry door there appears a timely reminder for the officiating minister that 'thy priests be clothed with righteousness'. It is a pity that such a warning was not more prominent in 1554, when the vicar was reported as a 'common sower of discord and dissension among his parishioners and a common slanderer of them'. He had given nothing to the church, had spent nothing at the Church Ale and had preached nothing from the pulpit for several years! At nearby Lilstock, a detour along a grassed track will bring you to the wonderfully atmospheric St Andrew's church. This diminutive place of worship – not in regular use for many years – has been lovingly restored by the Redundant Churches Trust, and is truly a place of solitude and reflection.

Wimbleball and Clatworthy Reservoirs

15 miles

Exmoor will not be everyone's idea of cycling heaven! High moorland – rising to over 1,700 feet above sea-level at Dunkery Beacon – and plunging valleys mean that it is more suited to experienced cyclists than mere mortals. The contrast with the excessively horizontal Somerset Levels, just a few miles to the east, could not be more marked. This aside, it is certainly an area of dramatic vistas and outstanding landscapes.

The villages are few and far between, and lie scattered around the valley bottoms, whilst the uplands are home to both deer and the indigenous Exmoor pony. With an above average level of rainfall, and numerous streams that flow down from the moorland heights, it comes as no surprise to discover vast reservoirs dotted across what is one of the country's smallest national parks, and two of them – Wimbleball Reservoir and Clatworthy Reservoir – feature on this cycle tour.

Map: OS Landranger 181 Minehead and the Brendon Hills (GR 974318).

Starting point: The picnic area at Bessom Cross alongside Wimbleball Reservoir. Follow the B3190 to Robbery Gate, 2½ miles west of Ralegh's Cross, before following the unclassified road signposted to Wimbleball Reservoir. On reaching the junction at Bessom Cross, turn left and then first right into the parking area.

Refreshments: Along the way, the only refreshment stop is the Ralegh's Cross Inn, although, being situated just 5 miles into the circuit, its pleasures probably appear a little too early along the way. A better option is to enjoy a picnic at journey's end in the picnic area alongside Wimbleball Reservoir.

The route: The 3¼ miles following 'B' roads in and around Ralegh's Cross have the potential to be quite busy, being some of the main thoroughfares across this part of Exmoor. This aside, the main challenge will prove to be the hills – there is a 300-foot ascent out of Clatworthy, for example, and a similar climb away from Wimbleball at the outset. This is not a circuit for the faint-hearted . . . but you should bear in mind the old adage about 'what goes up must come down'.

---

1. Leave the car park, and **turn L** to reach the road junction at Bessom Cross. **Turn R** – signposted to Watchet – and follow the road ahead for 2½ miles to its junction with the B3190 at Robbery Gate. **Turn L** – still signposted to Watchet – and follow the B3190 for 2½ miles to Ralegh's Cross and the Ralegh's Cross Inn. At this point,

Bessom Cross picnic site

keep directly ahead along the B3224 road – signposted to Taunton. Keep on this road for ¾ mile to a right turn signposted to Clatworthy.

2. Turn R, and keep on this side lane for 2 miles, to the junction at Forche's Cross. **Turn R** at this point, following the lane signposted to Clatworthy. In 1 mile, having passed Clatworthy church on the right, continue through this remote hamlet – ignoring a left turn marked 'unsuitable for heavy goods vehicles' – to the next junction. Follow the lane ahead – signposted to the reservoir viewing area. Continue ahead for ¾ mile to a

right turn signposted to Clatworthy Reservoir. This will prove to be an almost obligatory detour.

3. For the main route, keep directly ahead. Very shortly, ignore the lane ahead signposted to the fishing lodge, keeping instead to the 'main' lane that **bears L** to reach a junction in 150 yards. Follow the unmarked lane to the right, and continue for 1¼ miles to a minor crossroads. Continue ahead for a few yards to a T-junction, **turn R** and follow the road ahead for 1 mile to Sperry Cross and the B3190.

4. Cross this 'B' road and follow the lane opposite signposted to Brompton Regis. In 1½ miles, at the

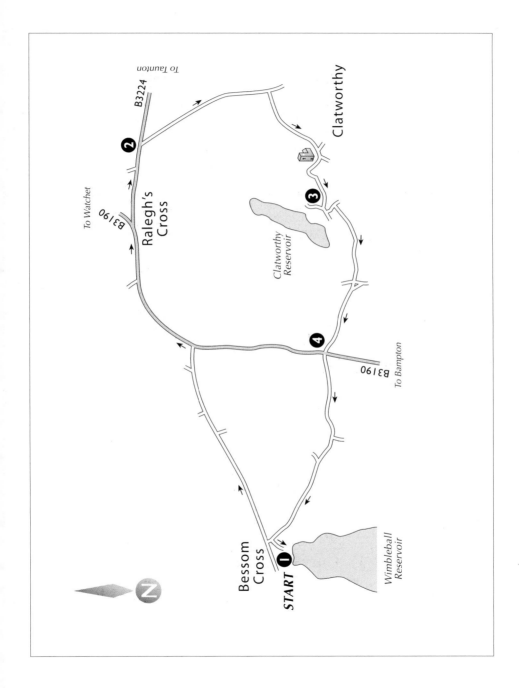

next junction, keep on the 'main' lane that **bears L**, still signposted to Brompton Regis. In ¼ mile, at the next junction, once again keep to the 'main' lane that **bears L**, all the while signposted to Brompton Regis. Follow this lane for 1¼ miles, down Rugg's Hill, to a **L turn** back into the Bessom Cross parking area alongside Wimbleball Reservoir.

●●●●●●●●●●●●●●●●●●●●●●●●●●

WIMBLEBALL RESERVOIR

Wimbleball Reservoir is the largest reservoir on Exmoor, extending over an area of 370 acres and with a capacity of 4,250 million gallons. Construction of the dam across the Haddeo Valley took place between November 1974 and December 1977, when filling commenced. In an area like Exmoor, there were fears and concerns for the environmental damage the project might cause, but careful landscaping, based upon plans drawn up by Dame Sylvia Crowe, has produced what is an asset for the National Park. To allay environmental concerns, the 160-foot high dam was even tinged pink to match the local stone! The reservoir supplies towns from Bridgwater and Taunton down to Tiverton and Exeter with their water, as well as being a major recreational amenity. There is fine fly-fishing on Wimbleball, for example, with an annual restocking of over 20,000 rainbow trout occurring. The record catch to date has been an 8½-pound specimen.

RALEGH'S CROSS

The Raleghs were an ancient family in this corner of Somerset, the family home being at Nettlecombe Court to the north of Monksilver. Ralegh's Cross takes its name from a funeral procession that rested here awhile when Simon Ralegh's body was being carried home to Nettlecombe Court. Today, the chief landmark at this lonely hilltop location is the Ralegh's Cross Inn; originally a drovers' staging post, it now profits from tourist traffic heading to and from Exmoor and the Somerset coast. The stone cross has gone, but the plinth remains to remind visitors of the significance of this spot in medieval times. There is also a reconstructed beacon, the original beacon having been part of that great chain that signalled the Armada on 19th July 1588.

CLATWORTHY

The little hamlet of Clatworthy lies hidden away along a network of winding lanes that only the most intrepid of motorists would seek out. The farms and cottages lie alongside the banks of the infant River Tone, which flows downstream to Taunton before its confluence with the Parrett at Burrowbridge. The once beautiful church has clearly seen better days, with decay and damp and peeling whitewash indicative of the high costs of maintaining rural churches. The headwaters of the Tone have been impounded to form the nearby Clatworthy Reservoir. Best known for its fine fishing, the 130 acres covered by this stretch of water are home to both rainbow and brown trout. The reservoir is also the site of a variety of natural habitats, including acid grassland, broadleaf woodland and scrub. The numerous inlets also present areas of damp marshland. These habitats are home to a rich array of wildfowl, with Canada goose, sparrowhawk, tawny owl, green woodpecker and grey wagtail as just a sample of the species found here all year round.

17

Wellington, Bradford-on-Tone and Milverton

21 miles

Taunton Deane is the area predominantly occupied by the middle reaches of the valley of the Tone, the river that flows from Clatworthy on Exmoor through Taunton to its confluence with the Parrett at Burrowbridge. A rolling tract of old-fashioned Somerset countryside, it lies neatly sandwiched between the Quantocks, the Brendons and the Black Downs, hills whose contours and slopes appear on the horizon at every turn. This is a fertile area, where tradition holds strong in the form of small fields, high hedgerows, rich pastureland and the occasional cider orchard. Around what is an undulating landscape lies a scattering of quiet villages and hamlets, whose impressive church towers stand as landmarks across the local landscape. From Bradford-on-Tone to Hillfarrance, from Milverton to Langford Budville, the settlements along the way all add interest and diversion. The hills are gentle, the atmosphere most relaxed – it is altogether a quite perfect place for a few hours' gentle cycling.

Map: OS Landranger 181 Minehead and the Brendon Hills (GR 138206).

Starting point: The North Street car park in the centre of Wellington. Follow the main road into the town centre – this was the A38 from Taunton to Exeter prior to the construction of a much-needed bypass – and, just south of the junction with the B3187, turn into the signposted car park.

Refreshments: Along the way are many opportunities for rest and refreshment. Wellington itself has a good number of pubs and cafes, whilst traditional hostelries can be found at Bradford-on-Tone, Allerford, Hillfarrance, Milverton, Langford Budville and Holywell Lake . . . this could turn into a veritable pub crawl! The Martlet in Langford Budville, with its open fires, inglenook, beams and flagstones, will prove especially inviting, with 16 of the circuit's 21 miles already under your belt.

The route: Other than having to negotiate a mile or two of fairly busy roads in and around Wellington, this cycle tour follows quiet lanes and byways in a sleepy corner of Taunton Deane. The landscape is undulating rather than flat, but none of the hills could be described as insurmountable. Most of the undulations feature on the section of the ride between Milverton and Holywell Lake.

Bradford-on-Tone

1. Exit the car park onto the B3187, and **turn R** up to its junction with the main street in Wellington – formerly the A38. **Turn L** at the traffic lights at this junction – signposted to Taunton – and follow the main road for ¾ mile to a left turn signposted to Nynehead. **Turn L** and follow this road for 1¼ miles through to a T-junction in Nynehead, where you **turn R** along the road signposted to Oake and Hillfarrance. Follow this road through an impressive sandstone gorge to the next junction, and keep on the road ahead signposted to Bradford. In 300 yards, take the **R turn** signposted to East Nynehead. Follow this lane for 1½ miles –

passing through East Nynehead – to a junction on the edge of Bradford-on-Tone.

2. **Turn R** into Bradford-on-Tone, before taking the **L turn** by the church, signposted to Hele and Taunton. In 250 yards, **turn L** along the lane to Hele and Allerford. Follow this lane through the scattered hamlet of Hele and, just past Hele Manor Farm, **turn L** at the turning to Allerford and Norton Fitzwarren. Cross the Tone, pass the Victory Inn and cross the level crossing in Allerford; at the next junction, take the **L turn** to Hillfarrance. At the next junction, 150 yards beyond Allerford Farm, **turn L** along the lane, again

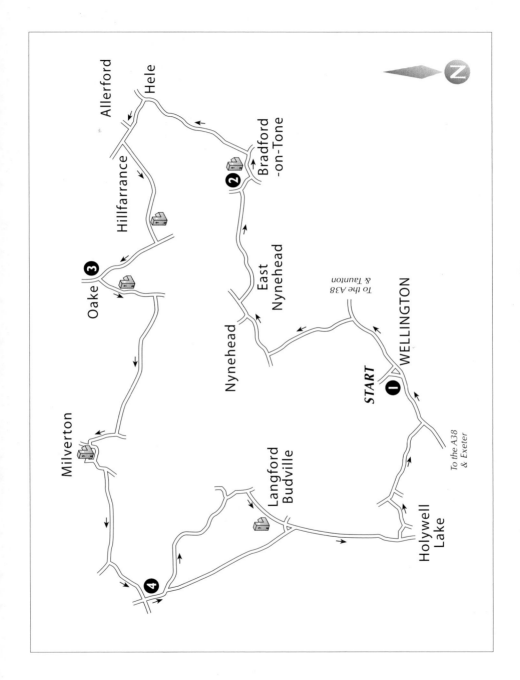

signposted to Hillfarrance. Follow this lane for 1½ miles to the next junction, passing through Hillfarrance along the way, before taking the **R turn** to Oake and Milverton.

3. Follow this road into Oake, and **turn L** just before the school along the road to Nynehead. Cycle down past the church on the left and, in 300 yards, just past the golf course, take the **R turn** to Milverton. In 2 miles, at a junction, take the **R turn**, again signposted to Milverton. Keep on this lane for 250 yards until it **bears L** up to Silver Street in Milverton. **Turn R**, then immediately **turn L** into North Street, before taking the first **L turn**, down St Michael's Hill – passing the church – to the junction with Sand Street. **Turn R** and, in 150 yards, **fork R** off the B3187 into Butts Way. Follow this road for 1 mile to a junction by Farthings Farm, and keep on the road ahead, signposted to Bathealton and Wellington, to a crossroads in ¾ mile.

4. **Turn L** – signposted to Wellington – and, in ¼ mile, **turn L** along an unsigned lane. Follow this secluded byway for 1½ miles to its junction with the B3187 in Chipley. **Turn R** and, in 300 yards, **turn R** again along the turning to Langford Budville. Cycle through this village, passing the church and pub, before keeping ahead at a minor crossroads to reach a junction. Keep ahead on the 'main'

road, signposted to Holywell Lake. Follow this road for 1½ miles and, immediately before Holywell Public House, **turn L** along the lane to Payton and Weling. In 150 yards, at the next junction, **turn L** and continue for 600 yards into Payton. Keep on the 'main' lane at a junction – it **bears R** – and once again keep on the 'main' lane at the next junction, this time **bearing L**. Follow the road for another mile to the former A38 – the Exeter Road – in Wellington. Turn L towards the town centre and, in another ¾ mile, **turn L** into the North Street car park.

● ●

WELLINGTON

For decades, Wellington was best known for being an appalling bottleneck on the A38 trunk road into Devon and Cornwall. With the arrival of a bypass and subsequently the M5 motorway, the town has become a rather more pleasant place to explore. Wellington Museum, housed in a 17th-century posting house, reflects the history of the town, whilst the town hall was given a classical façade when it was built in 1833. Wellington's most famous son, Sir John Popham, was variously Solicitor and Attorney General, Chief Justice and Speaker of the House of Commons. He was also involved in the trials of Mary Queen of Scots, Sir Walter Raleigh and the Gunpowder plotters. His earthly remains lie in a free-standing tomb with a towering Corinthian canopy in Wellington's 15th-century church. As with so many churches in the area, its chief feature is a handsome pinnacled tower.

NYNEHEAD

At the time of Domesday, Nynehead belonged to the Bishops of Winchester and was known as 'Nichehede'. It is a sleepy little place, with a quiet tempo, one commentator describing its atmosphere on summer evenings as having 'the sensation of deep, concentrated greenness like a cocoon'. Heading east from the village is a memorable experience, as the lane cuts through a sandstone gorge known as 'Nynehead Hollow'. Steep banks of red sandstone, overshadowed by hanging trees, create the atmosphere of a cave or passage through a canyon. This cut was the work of the Sanfords, who came to Nynehead Court in 1600. A bust to John and Henrietta Sanford can be seen in a chapel in the village's All Saints' church.

BRADFORD-ON-TONE

As with many other settlements bearing the same name, Bradford was originally a 'broad ford' through the local river, in this case the Tone. The 15th-century bridge, with its pointed arches, has its origins in these Saxon times. The main body of the village, including St Giles' church and the White Horse Inn, stands on a shoulder of land above the river. St Giles', originally Norman, was the subject of many alterations in the 15th and 16th centuries. Its solid looking Perpendicular style is typical of this part of the country, although the combination of local grey sandstone, Hamstone and Black Down

chert used in its construction may come as a surprise. The well-preserved stocks in the churchyard are worth seeking out, as is the old village pump preserved in a niche near the village hostelry.

MILVERTON

Milverton, originally known as 'Mill Ford settlement', presents the appearance of a quite genteel place, whose streets – with names such as Butts Way and Archery Close – evoke images of far earlier times. Its tannery had a college for apprentices and its cobbles would have sounded to the noise of many a boisterous pair of feet. This was the birthplace of Thomas Young, the initiator of the Rosetta Stone decipherment. In a former guise, Milverton was also a weaving town, whose wealth and prosperity are evident in the many handsome properties that line the streets around the church. The weavers became famous for their serges, druggets and baizes, although the coming of the steam age saw the industry decline as competition from Lancashire and Yorkshire mills led to bankruptcies locally. Milverton has – quite rightly – been described as an 'aristocrat among small settlements'. When you see its Georgian properties enhanced by the use of rugged red sandstone, it is not difficult to see why.

Langport, Somerton and Muchelney

18 miles

This ride finds the cyclist deep in the South Somerset countryside, in a landscape often described as 'Hamstone Country'. The name comes from the coppery-brown stone quarried on nearby Ham Hill that forms the building blocks of so many of the local properties. This is a part of the county dominated by historic settlements, including villages such as Muchelney and Long Sutton, and ancient towns such as Langport and Somerton, all set amidst the rolling hills of South Somerset.

The northern part of the circuit, above the main A372, crosses an undulating landscape, whilst to the south of the main road the route returns to the moors. A network of drainage ditches and artificial cuts, whose existence prevents this corner of the county reverting to primeval bog, crosses this lowland part of the county. This most evocative of landscapes, almost devoid of contour lines, makes for almost perfect cycling country. An added attraction at journey's end is the all too short River Parrett Cycleway, a short stretch of off-road cycling that follows the trackbed of the former Langport to Yeovil railway.

Maps: OS Landranger 193 Taunton and Lyme Regis (GR 414265). A very short section of the circuit creeps on to OS Landranger 182 Weston-super-Mare.

Starting point: The River Parrett Visitor Centre in Langport. At the western end of Langport's main street, the A372 crosses the River Parrett. Immediately west of the river bridge, turn into the Westover Trading Estate, and the Visitor Centre is on the immediate left-hand side.

Refreshments: Both Langport and Somerton can offer a good number of pubs and cafes for refreshment, although the best resting place along the way is Long Sutton. Here, in the centre of the village, overlooking the green, is the Devonshire Arms, a tall, gabled and solid stone inn with a cosily old-fashioned front bar and an adjoining restaurant. This is the perfect spot to rest and linger awhile, with all of the – albeit gentle – gradients but a distant memory and just easy cycling between here and journey's end.

The route: Other than a mile or two of relatively busy roads in Langport and Somerton, this circuit follows quiet lanes and byways in the south of the county. The main A372 does have to be crossed on one occasion south of Somerton, but this is the only encounter with significant traffic volumes outside of the towns. The early part of the route has its occasional ups and downs but, once the ancient village of Long Sutton is left behind, it is idyllic cycling all of the way.

The market cross at Somerton dates from the 17th century

1. Leave the car park alongside the River Parrett Visitor Centre, **turn L** and, at the end of the trading estate, **fork L** onto the Parrett Cycleway. Continue for 200 yards to a junction, and **turn L** to follow Huish Drove. In ¾ mile, cross the River Parrett and continue along a quiet back lane to a junction. **Turn L** and, at the next junction, **turn R** and cycle past St Mary's church before joining the A372. **Turn L**, and follow the A372 for ¾ mile, passing Huish Episcopi school and crossing a railway line before reaching a crossroads. Cross over into Wearne Lane, signposted to Wearne. In 600 yards, at a T-junction, **turn R** and cycle through Wearne and on to the next junction. **Turn L** – signposted to Low Ham and High Ham – and, in 100 yards, at the top of a climb, **turn R** along the lane to Pitney. In ¾ mile, just before reaching Pitney, **turn L** along the lane signposted to Park. Follow this lane for 3½ miles to join the B3153 in Somerton, passing through Park along the way.

2. Turn L on to the B3153 and, in 200 yards, at the mini-roundabout by the Royal Oak Inn, **turn R** into the town centre. In 300 yards, in the Market Place, **bear R** by the White Hart Inn, pass the Globe Inn and continue along Kirkham Street to reach the police station on the left. At this point, **bear R** down

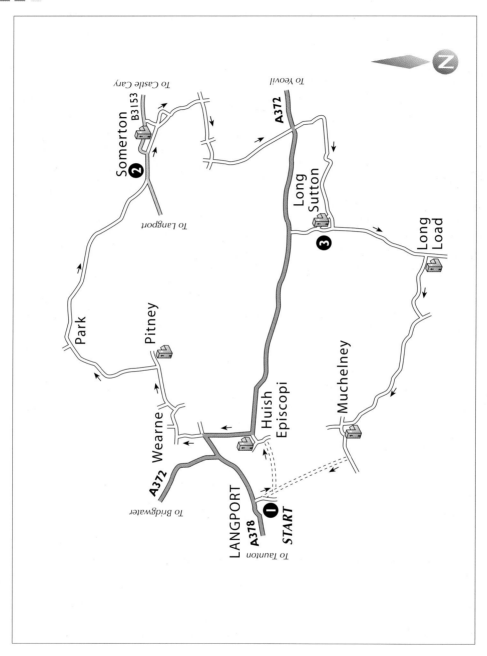

Parsonage Hill to a mini-roundabout; **turn L** and continue for ½ mile to a crossroads at Ashen Cross. **Turn R**, and head across the hilltop for ¾ mile to the second crossroads, at Badgers Cross. **Turn L**, and follow the lane in a southerly direction for 1¼ miles to the A372. Cross over – waymarked to Bineham – and, in 600 yards, keep on the main lane as it **bears R** – signposted to Knole and Long Sutton. In ½ mile, in the village of Knole, keep on the main lane through the village, ignoring all side turns. Continue for ¾ mile to a junction on the edge of Long Sutton and, keeping to the main lane, which **bears R**, continue downhill to a junction with the B3165 in Long Sutton by the Devonshire Arms.

3. **Turn L** – signposted to Martock – and head south for 1½ miles into Little Load and Long Load. Pass the Crown Inn, before you **turn R** by the church – no waymark – to follow a side lane for ¾ mile down to a T-junction on Wet Moor. **Turn R**, and continue for 1¾ miles through Muchelney Ham to a junction, where you **turn R** into Muchelney. On reaching the green by the church, keep left along the road signposted to Drayton and Curry Rival. Cycle out of Muchelney, crossing the Parrett, and – having passed the abutments of the derelict local railway – **turn sharp R** to join the Parrett Cycleway. Follow this off-road cyclepath north for 1¼ miles to a gate on the southern edge of Langport and a junction. **Turn R** and, in 20 yards, **turn L** to retrace the route along the final section of the cyclepath back to the Westover Trading Estate and the River Parrett Visitor Centre.

• •

LANGPORT and HUISH EPISCOPI

Without any doubt, Langport owes its prosperity to the River Parrett. In centuries past, this was a navigable waterway, along whose course would come boatloads of coal and lime, salt and fish. It was the river which gave inspiration and birth to the merchanting and banking enterprise of the Stuckeys and the Bagehots, which dictated so much of Somerset's economy. Running east from the river is Bow Street, the main road through the town, resting upon a causeway built by the Romans. This elevation was crucial, given the susceptibility of the Parrett to bursting its banks and flooding much of the surrounding lowland. The church of All Saints has one of those soaring towers so typical of Somerset. The church dates from the 15th century, although it retains a stone relief from the former Norman place of worship on the site. One of the town's more recent attractions is the River Parrett Visitor Centre. The displays relate not only to the river and its former waterborne trade, but also to the flora and fauna of the surrounding moors. Adjoining Langport, and formerly a more important settlement, is Huish Episcopi. The church in Huish has one of the finest towers in the West Country. It is divided into stages by horizontal bands of quatrefolds and is adorned with an array of pinnacles, niches and elaborate battlements.

SOMERTON

Somerton, the old capital of Somerset, was destroyed by Ethelbald, King of Mercia, in AD 732, and again by the Danes in AD 877. This ancient settlement is centred upon the market place, where a fine battlemented market cross, dating from the 17th century, faces the square. The whole is surrounded by the old town hall, Georgian houses with the occasional Hamstone mullioned window and crowned by the church to the north. St Michael's is a mixture of several building ages, and includes a fine 15th-century roof, the original building dating from the 13th century. Nearby, Broad Street, wide and handsome, is tree lined and as such is reminiscent of a French boulevard. In the same part of the town, some of the more notable buildings include the Old Parsonage, with its 17th-century façade and oriel window, Somerton Court, whose fine porch and mullioned windows date from 1641, and the Hext Almshouses of 1626.

LONG SUTTON

Writing in 1938, S P B Mais commented, 'I saw in front of me the first of the massive tall church towers that form so conspicuous a feature of the Somerset scenery. It was Long Sutton, and the first thing to be said about Long Sutton is that it is very long indeed.' The tower in question is all of 96 feet and 3 inches high, with fine Somerset tracery and the date of its repair – 1622 – on the belfry window. Internally, a coloured wooden pulpit of the mid-15th century, bearing the initials of John Petherton, Abbot of

Athelney, will catch the eye. The church towers above the green, which lies at the crossing point of the ancient route from Somerton to Martock with the Ilchester to Langport byway. Around the green stand many fine buildings, including the Victorian Devonshire Arms and the local manor house behind its protective hedgerows.

MUCHELNEY

Muchelney literally means 'big island', a name derived from the fact that the village stands a few feet higher than the surrounding Levels, which in centuries past would have been damp marshland. Benedictine monks established the abbey, destroyed during the Dissolution of the Monasteries, in the 8th century. Today, little more than the ground plan remains for visitors to explore. It was never a large establishment, 20 monks being the maximum recorded at the abbey, with only 10 remaining in 1539. After the Dissolution, the building's masonry apparently became fair game for the local villagers, and it is an intriguing task to spot the finials and carvings that now adorn local cottages and farmhouses. Opposite the village church – most noted for its ceiling painting depicting buxom cherubs floating on cotton-wool clouds – is the Priest's House. This is a delightful survival from the monastic days, a late medieval two-storeyed thatched cottage, with a fine two-centred doorway and a four-light transom window. Despite its lack of size, this dwelling is modelled upon the design of a large mansion.

Langport, Fivehead and Athelney

19 miles

The Somerset Levels, described most succinctly by one commentator as 'an excessively horizontal landscape', is divided into two distinct regions by the low ridge of the Polden Hills. To the north of the Poldens lies the Vale of Avalon, whilst to the south lie the vast open spaces of Sedgemoor, a landscape that was in centuries past nothing more than waterlogged, low-lying marshland. Extensive drainage has left the area with a dense network of rhynes, drainage ditches and watercourses, the perfect habitat for moisture-loving plants and wildfowl.

Scattered across this low-lying area of Somerset are a number of villages and hamlets, each with much to catch the eye. These range from the former mill at Hambridge to the old churches at Isle Brewers and Fivehead, as well as the Willows and Wetlands Visitor Centre at Meare Green and the tidal waters of the River Parrett at Stathe and Oath. There is also Athelney, with its historic associations with King Alfred and those cakes – legend set deep in the ancient heart of Somerset.

Map: OS Landranger 193 Taunton to Lyme Regis (GR 414265).

Starting point: The River Parrett Visitor Centre in Langport. At the western end of Langport's main street, the A378 crosses the River Parrett. Immediately west of the river bridge, turn into the Westover Trading Estate, and the Visitor Centre is on the immediate left-hand side.

Refreshments: Along the way, there are inns at Drayton, Hambridge, North Curry, Oath and at journey's end in Langport. Perhaps of greater interest will be the Willows and Wetlands Visitor Centre at Meare Green, where, in addition to interpretive displays, visitors can enjoy the delights of a traditional English cream tea.

The route: Other than a couple of brief encounters with the A378 – at Langport and again near Curry Mallet – this cycle tour follows quiet lanes and byways across the ancient landscape of West Sedgemoor. The terrain is generally level, with just the occasional hill around Curry Mallet and North Curry. There is the added bonus of a short section of traffic-free cyclepath at the start of the ride south of Langport.

---

1. Leave the car park, **turn L** and, towards the end of the Westover Trading Estate, **fork L** onto the Parrett Cycleway. Follow this track down to Huish Drove, **turn R** and then shortly **turn L** to join the next section of the cyclepath. Follow this path in a southerly

An ancient bridge crosses the river at Isle Brewers

direction for 1½ miles to a gated exit point alongside a cottage, before you **bear R** down to a lane. **Turn R**, and follow this lane for 1¼ miles into Drayton. Just past the Drayton Arms and the church, **turn L** into School Lane and, in another ½ mile, in Whitecross, keep on the main lane as it **bears R** to head towards Hambridge. Follow this lane for 1 mile to the B3168, **turn L** and continue for 1½ miles into Hambridge itself. Immediately before the village school, **turn R** at the turning for Isle Brewers and Fivehead.

2. In 1½ miles, at a crossroads, **turn R** towards Isle Brewers and Fivehead and continue for 2½ miles into Fivehead. At the junction

before the church, keep ahead along the road signposted to Curry Mallet. Having passed the church, keep left in front of the village hall and, in 150 yards, **turn R** to Curry Mallet. Continue into Curry Mallet and, 175 yards past the village sign, **turn R** by a whitewashed thatched property onto the North Curry road. In ½ mile, at a junction, **turn R**, then almost immediately **turn L** towards North Curry, before descending Rock Hill to reach the A378. **Turn R** and, in ½ mile, **turn L** towards North Curry. Follow what becomes a winding lane for 2 miles up to a junction in North Curry.

3. **Turn R**, and continue for 2¼ miles until you **turn L** in Meare

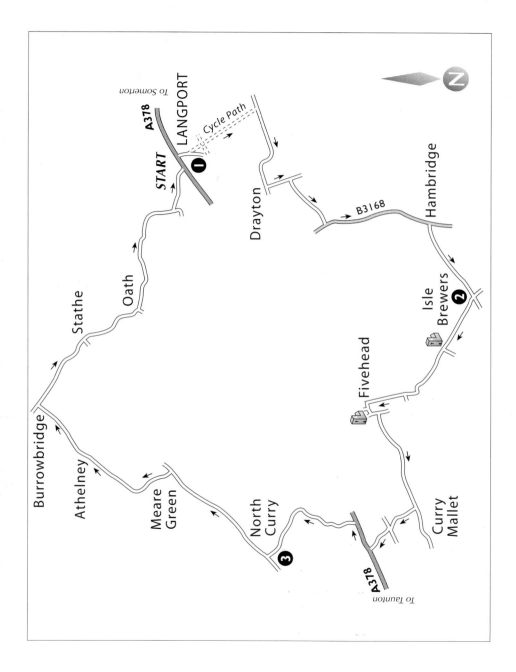

Green down a lane waymarked to Athelney. Follow this lane for 3 miles, passing through Athelney, to a junction on the fringes of Burrowbridge. **Turn R** – signposted to Oath, Stathe and Langport – and follow the road for 2½ miles to the Black Smock Inn at Oath. Shortly after this public house, ignore the right turn and continue ahead towards Wick and Langport. In 1½ miles, having reached Wick, keep on the lane as it **bears L** and continue for ¾ mile to the A378. **Turn L**, and head into Langport, where the first **R turn** will return you to the Westover Trading Estate and the River Parrett Visitor Centre.

• •

DRAYTON

With its pleasing vistas of tile, thatch and twining roses, Drayton has earned the praises of many a guidebook writer. Standing on a low ridge that stretches from Langport like a spine to join up in time with the foothills of the Blackdowns, most visitors are attracted by the delights of St Catherine's church. Amongst the features to look out for are the fine Perpendicular tower and an ancient churchyard cross that bears a carving of St Michael and the dragon.

NORTH CURRY

North Curry, with its magnificent church, terraces of cottages, large houses and the delightful Queen's Square, is indeed a handsome place. The church, cruciform in layout with a central octagonal tower, contains a marble plaque that relates the story of the Reeve's Feast. This was held on Boxing Day until 1868, and commemorated the granting of a charter

by King John to hold a local market. An effigy of the king was placed on the festive table to ornament a huge mince pie, and revellers were able to drink at the Reeve's expense until a pair of candles of one pound weight were burned out. Queen's Square marks the point where several roads converge around a garden space, with a flagpole and slender cross standing on the five hexagonal steps erected to commemorate the 24 men of the village killed in the Great War.

ATHELNEY

Athelney stands at the centre of an area where willows are grown for basket weavers. At the height of this trade in the late 19th century, over 2,000 acres of the local moors were used for withy beds. The willows are cut each spring, when visitors will notice the bundles of withies gathered into heaps in the local fields. Just off the route in Athelney, an obelisk marks the location where King Alfred built a priory after being saved from the Danes by hiding on the bleak and desolate moors.

THE RIVER PARRETT

The Parrett, flowing to the Bristol Channel just downstream of Bridgwater, has been used for navigation since time immemorial, serving the villages and hamlets in and around Langport. The Parrett Navigation Company was established in 1836 to construct a series of locks, as well as extending navigation to Westport by means of a 2-mile cut. It provided an important outlet for local agricultural produce as well as a means of supplying Welsh coal to the area, but navigation was abandoned in 1878, due to inevitable competition from the newly constructed railway network.

South Petherton and Ilminster

19 miles

Deep in the South Somerset countryside, this cycle tour explores a corner of the county that appears to be dominated by market towns and grand country houses. This is a landscape of gentle winding lanes and warm stone from Ham Hill, of undulations and the occasional rolling hillside. The huge coppery-brown slabs of hamstone have been planed and shaped over many generations to provide the building-blocks for churches and mansions, tombs and statues, gateposts and stiles. Evidence of this lies everywhere along the way, from the charming cottages of South Petherton to the packhorse bridge at Dowlish Wake, and from Ilminster's handsome church to the welcoming Poulett Arms in Hinton St George. Set amongst a traditional agricultural landscape of scattered small farms and high hedgerows, this is very much a journey through what visitors would perceive as the archetypal Somerset landscape.

Map: OS Landranger 193 Taunton and Lyme Regis (GR 433169)

Starting point: St James Street car park in South Petherton. Leave the nearby A303 and head northwards into this large village. Turn left at the second mini-roundabout into Knapp Hill – signposted to the village centre – and at the bottom of the hill the car park lies on the right-hand side.

Refreshments: Visitors will be spoiled for choice when it comes to refreshment facilities along the way, with several inns that feature regularly in the *Good Pub Guide*. Chief amongst these are the Poulett Arms in Hinton St George and the New Inn at Dowlish Wake. There are also welcoming hostelries at Ilminster, Shepton Beauchamp and South Petherton. If you prefer the 'cup which cheers but doth not inebriate', then Minstrels Coffee Shop in Ilminster will prove a delight with its teas and coffees and delicious homemade cakes.

The route: There are only two places along the way where real care and caution need to be exercised. At the outset, a busy roundabout on the A303 has to be negotiated, whilst the streets of Ilminster are always busy with local traffic. Other than these locations, the route follows quiet lanes and byways across the rolling landscape of South Somerset. There are a number of climbs along the way – mainly between Dinnington and Barrington – but none of these hills is of any great distance or duration.

Dillington House, near Ilminster

1. Leave the car park, **turn L** up Knapp Hill to a mini-roundabout, where you **turn R** and cycle for ½ mile to a major roundabout on the A303. Take the second exit from this roundabout – signposted to Yeabridge. Follow this lane in a southerly direction, passing through Yeabridge, to a junction by Yeabridge Farm. **Turn R** – this lane is unmarked – and continue for 600 yards to a junction in Over Stratton. Follow the 'main' road ahead – signposted to Merriott and Crewkerne – and then to the left. Continue in a southerly direction for 1½ miles to a junction with Church Street in Merriott; **turn R** and continue to a T-junction. **Turn R** – signposted to Martock and Ilchester – and, in 100 yards, take the **L turn** to Hinton St George and Dinnington. Follow this road for 1 mile into Hinton St George.

2. Cycle through the village, passing the Poulett Arms, before keeping right along the main road that **bears R** by the village cross, up past the church. Continue following this road as it winds its way downhill into Dinnington. In this hamlet, take the **second L turn** to Kingstone and Ilminster. Cycle up what is a sunken lane to a junction; keep ahead for 100 yards to a fork, where you **bear R** before continuing for 600 yards to a hilltop junction. Follow the main road ahead and, in 250 yards,

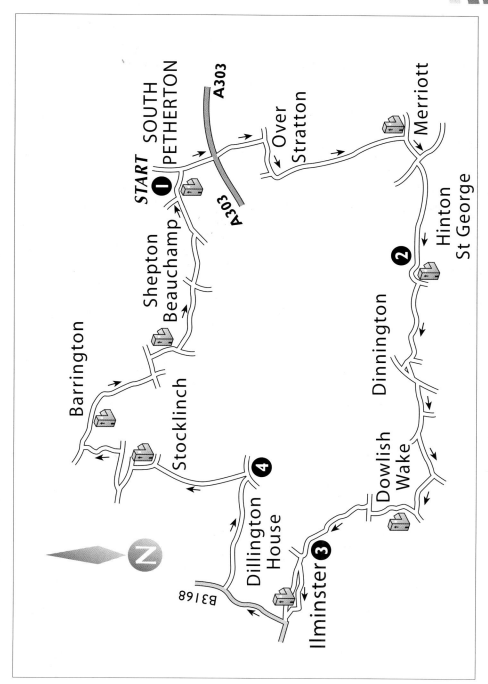

SOUTH PETHERTON

START ❶

A303

A303

Over Stratton

Merriott

Shepton Beauchamp

Hinton St George

❷

Barrington

Dinnington

Stocklinch

❹

Dowlish Wake

Dillington House

❸ Ilminster

B3168

N

fork **L** along the lane to Chillington and Cudworth. In ½ mile, take the **R turn** to Dowlish Wake. At the junction by the Dower House in Dowlish Wake, keep ahead, climbing up past the church before continuing for ½ mile to a junction in Kingstone. **Turn R** – signposted to Ilminster – and, at a junction in just 30 yards, **turn L** towards Ilminster. Follow this road for 1 mile to its junction with the former A303 in Ilminster – the current A303 bypasses the town – by the White Horse.

3. **Turn L** and, in 100 yards, **fork L** along the road leading to the town centre. Cycle through the High Street, passing the church, before you **bear R** along what is called Silver Street and then **bear L** along West Street to its junction with the former A303. **Turn L**, pass the Crown Inn and, in 100 yards, **turn R** onto the B3168, signposted to Curry Rivel and Langport. Climb out of Ilminster and, in ¾ mile, **turn R** along the private driveway to Dillington House. In 600 yards, just before the mansion, **bear L**, **then R**, to pass the house on the right before continuing along the driveway for ¾ mile up to a junction with the former A303 by a thatched property called the Lodge.

4. **Turn L**, then almost immediately **turn L** again, along the lane to Stocklinch. Follow this lane for 1¼ miles to a junction on the edge of Stocklinch. **Keep L** along the main lane, cycle past the church to a junction; **turn L** and continue for ¼ mile along Tunway to the next junction. Take a sharp **R turn** – there is no waymark – and cycle uphill for ½ mile to the next junction. **Turn L**, and cycle downhill to a junction in Barrington by a children's play area. **Turn R**, and cycle through Barrington for 1½ miles to a minor crossroads just beyond the top of a climb. **Turn L**, and follow a lane downhill to a junction in Shepton Beauchamp by the Duke of York. **Turn R** along Church Street for ¼ mile before taking a **L turn** into Washcross Lane. Follow this lane for 1 mile to a crossroads; cross straight over and continue for ½ mile to a junction. **Turn L**, and in ½ mile the lane reaches a junction in South Petherton. Follow the road ahead towards Yeovil and, by the Methodist church, keep on the main road as it **bears R** into the centre of South Petherton. This is St James Street, which is followed for 200 yards back to the car park on the left.

●●●●●●●●●●●●●●●●●●●●●●●●

SOUTH PETHERTON

South Petherton translates as 'the farmstead by the Parrett', one of Somerset's best known rivers, flowing just to the east of this small town. In former times this was a settlement of some importance, being the location of both a royal palace and a mission centre in the Saxon era. Today, South Petherton is a most pleasant place, with its fine church standing amongst steep streets and narrow stepped alleys, the elegant spire that rises above the octagonal tower dominating the town's skyline. Inside, there is a rather grand effigy, dating from the 13th century, to Sir William de Albini. What is more remarkable is that this effigy only came to light during groundworks for a petrol storage tank at a nearby garage! Thomas Coke, the noted Methodist preacher, was a former curate at the church, but his radical pronouncements led to his being hounded out of the town by the proverbial mob.

HINTON ST GEORGE

Hinton St George is the ancestral seat of the Poulett family, descended from Hercules, Lord of Tournon in Picardy. One of the family married Elizabeth Deneband, whose own family had been Lords of Hinton since the days of Henry III. This is a pleasant settlement, with a village cross set against a backdrop of thatched cottages; a place of wide streets and diminutive sweet-smelling gardens. The highlight of the village is without doubt the fine church. To quote one local guidebook: 'To enter Hinton church and see the colossal monuments in the transept is one of the memorable experiences of Somerset. Great towering riots of carving where figures, curtains, columns, coats-of-arms, scrolls and urns join in one visual cacophony of splendour.' The monuments are all dedicated to the Poulett family, whose influence within Hinton St George even extends to the village hostelry – known as the Poulett Arms.

ILMINSTER and DILLINGTON HOUSE

The construction of a bypass that carries the heavy volume of traffic following the A303 from London to the southwest made Ilminster altogether a better place. The centre of the town is the attractive market place, where the shops lie grouped around the open-sided market hall, which dates from 1813. Overshadowing the whole scene is the

lofty Perpendicular tower of St Mary's church, a place of worship that was founded as far back as the 7th century by King Ine. This magnificent construction, with its carved parapet, rich tracery and pinnacles, is evidence of the prosperity found in the locality in the Middle Ages. In the 18th century, the town's fortunes were based upon gloving and weaving, industries that took advantage of the raw materials provided by local farmers. The George Hotel in the town has a certain claim to fame. A plaque announces that this was the first hotel in which Queen Victoria stayed. Although not strictly true – Victoria was merely a princess at the time and was staying in the town with her mother – it certainly puts the George on the map! To the north of Ilminster, the route passes Dillington House. This grand mansion, of largely 19th-century construction but with 17th-century wings, was home to the Speke family – and for a time was the residence of Lord North. Today, the complex is owned by Somerset County Council and is run as an adult education centre.

BARRINGTON

Barrington has a rambling main street lined with thatched cottages and gabled farms that are centred on a fine old inn. Above all, the village is known for Barrington House, a grand National Trust property that dates back to the 16th century. Today, it stands as one of the best examples of 1920s creativity, having been extensively renovated by a Colonel A A Lyle. It is a model estate, with its own complex of farm buildings, landscaped grounds and a large kitchen garden. Barrington is the archetypal English mansion, with Elizabethan gables and twisty chimneys, as well as 'enough mullions, transoms and lights to reduce an apprentice window-cleaner to a state of permanent whimpering dementia', to quote one local guidebook.

ROUTE GRADINGS

These subjective rankings are based upon such factors as the severity of the gradients and traffic volumes.

EASY CIRCUITS

1. Along the Bristol and Bath Railway Path.
7. Wedmore and Brent Knoll.
9. Burtle and the Polden Ridge.
10. Glastonbury, Shapwick Heath and Westhay Moor.
11. Street and Baltonsborough.
12. Burrowbridge and Bridgwater.
18. Langport, Somerton and Muchelney.
19. Langport, Fivehead and Athelney.

MODERATE CIRCUITS

2. Ashton Court, Pill and the Avon Gorge
8. Cannington and Steart.
13. Castle Cary, Ditcheat and Lydford.
15. Nether Stowey and Lilstock.
17. Wellington, Bradford-on-Tone and Milverton.
20. South Petherton and Ilminster.

STRENUOUS CIRCUITS

3. Bath, Freshford and Wellow.
4. Cheddar and the Mendip Hills.
5. Mells, Nunney and Great Elm.
6. Oakhill, Binegar and Leigh upon Mendip.
14. Williton and the Quantock Hills.
16. Wimbleball and Clatworth Reservoirs.